SOLDIER TO ADVOCATE: C. E. S. WOOD'S 1877 LEGACY

A SOLDIER'S UNPUBLISHED DIARY, DRAWINGS, POETRY, AND LETTERS OF ALASKA AND THE NEZ PERCE CONFLICT

BY
GEORGE VENN

Wordcraft of Oregon, LLC

THE GRANDE RONDE VALLEY
LA GRANDE, OREGON

Wordcraft of Oregon, LLC, La Grande, Oregon 97850
© 2006 by George Venn. All rights reserved
Printed in the United States of America

Library of Congress Control Number: 2006928130

ISBN: 1-877655-48-1
ISBN: 978-1-877655-48-7

CONTENTS

Credits and Illustrations	v-viii
Introduction	2-3
Part I. The Explorer: I Do Not Wish to Loaf about Sitka	4-21
Part II. The Soldier's Diary: Facing the Probabilities by Writing	22-55
Part III. The Advocate: His Drawings, Poems, and Prose	56-79
Part IV. The Writer: A Legacy of Family, Friendship, and Justice	80-92
Acknowledgments	94-96

COVER:

Background: "Chief Joseph's Band, Lapwai, Idaho, Spring, 1877." Roy Berk Collection. Courtesy of Northwest Museum of Arts and Culture/Eastern Washington Historical Society, Spokane, Washington

"Lt. C.E.S. Wood, June 6, 1878." Reproduced by permission of Wood Collection, The Huntington Library, San Marino, California

"Chief Joseph, October, 1877." Reproduced by permission of the Washington State Historical Society, Tacoma.

OTHER WORKS BY GEORGE VENN

West of Paradise (1999)
>poetry collection

Pulling Together (1997)
>Baker County anthology with Primus St. John

River Hills Rounded With Wind (1997)
>Wasco County anthology with Paulann Petersen

Talking On Paper: An Anthology of Oregon Letters and Diaries (1994)
>historical anthology with Shannon Applegate & Terence O'Donnell

The Stories We Tell: An Anthology of Oregon Folk Literature (1994)
>historical anthology with Suzi Jones & Jarold Ramsey

From Here We Speak: An Anthology of Oregon Poetry (1993)
>historical anthology with Ingrid Wendt & Primus St. John

The World Begins Here: An Anthology of Oregon Short Fiction (1993)
>historical anthology with Glen Love

Many Faces: An Anthology of Oregon Autobiography (1993)
>historical anthology with Stephen Dow Beckham

Varieties of Hope: An Anthology of Oregon Prose (1993)
>historical anthology with Gordon Dodds

Marking the Magic Circle (1987)
>essays, fiction, poetry, Chinese translations, and Jan Boles photos.

Oregon East Magazine 1950-1985 (1986)
>college anthology with Ron Ragsdale, Bill Stafford, Bill Kittredge

Off the Main Road (1978)
>poetry collection

Sunday Afternoon: Grande Ronde (1975)
>poetry chapbook

Eastern Oregon Literary Supplement (1972, 1973, 1974)
>regional newspapers annual anthology

CREDITS/LIST OF ILLUSTRATIONS

PART I. THE EXPLORER

1. Plate 1.1: "Second Lieutenant Charles Erskine Scott Wood, June 6, 1878." Reproduced by permission of Wood Collection, The Huntington Library, San Marino, California.

5. Plate 1.2: "Lt. C. E. S. Wood, West Point, 1874, Graduation." Reproduced by permission of Wood Collection, The Huntington Library, San Marino, California.

6. Plate 1.3: "Miss Nanny Moale Smith, 1872." Courtesy of J. Kirkham and Patty Johns Collection.

7. Plate 1.4: "Lt. C. E. S. Wood, Ft. Vancouver, 1877." Reproduced by permission of Wood Collection, The Huntington Library, San Marino, California.

8. Plate 1.5: "Mrs. Nanny Smith Wood, Portland, 1879." Courtesy of the Erskine Wood Collection, Aubrey Watzek Library Special Collections, Lewis & Clark College, Portland, Oregon.

9. Plate 1.6: "General O. O. Howard." *New York Daily Graphic*, August 3, 1877. Courtesy of The The Chicago Research Library.

10. Letter: O. O. Howard to C. E. S. Wood, April 5, 1877. Reprinted courtesy of the Erskine Wood Collection, Aubrey Watzek Library Special Collections, Lewis & Clark College, Portland, Oregon.

11. Plate 1.7: "Taylor Expedition in Sitka." Courtesy of the Erskine Wood Collection, Aubrey Watzek Library Special Collections, Lewis & Clark College, Portland, Oregon.

12-13. Letter: C. E. S. Wood to O. O. Howard, May 16, 1877. Reprinted courtesy of the Oliver Otis Howard Papers, George J. Mitchell Department of Special Collections & Archives, Bowdoin College Library, Brunswick, Maine.

14. Plate 1.8: "The Indian Village at Sitka." *Century* XXIV, 1882, 324.

14. Plate 1.9: "Yakutat Natives in Potlatch Dancing Costumes. Sitka, Alaska..." c. 1904. Alaska State Library, Case and Draper Collection, P39-0786.

15-17. Plates 1.10–1.12: "Thlinkit Woman.(Sitka Kwahn)," "Song of the Salmon Fishing," and "The Main Street of Sitka" all courtesy of *Century* XXIV, 324-338.

18. Plate 1.13: "Interior of Chief Klart-Reech's House, Chilkat, Alaska." c. 1895. Alaska State Library, Winter and Pond Collection, P87-0010.

18. Plate 1.14: "U. S. Army Headquarters, Sitka, Alaska." ca. 1868-69. Alaska State Library, Eadweard Muybridge Photo, Sitka-Russian Buildings, 01.

19. Plate 1.15: "Chief Lawyer, ca. 1861." Courtesy of University of Washington Libraries, Special Collections, NA627.

20. Plate 1.16: "Chief Joseph's Band, Lapwai, Idaho, Spring, 1877." Courtesy of Northwest Museum of Arts and Culture/Eastern Washington Historical Society, Spokane, Washington.

21. Plate 1.17: "Nez Perces' Route from Oregon to Canada, 1877." Map reprinted from Jerome Greene's *Nez Perce Summer 1877* (Helena: Montana Historical Society Press, 2000: 9). Courtesy of Montana Historical Society Press.

PART II. THE SOLDIER

23. Plate 2.1: C. E. S. Wood's Diary page for May, 1877. Reprinted by permission of Wood Collection, The Huntington Library, San Marino, California.

26. Plate 2.2: "Sitka Harbor, U.S. Navy or Coast Guard Longboats, 1878." M. M. Hazeltine Photo, Oregon Historical Society, #OrHi27819.

27. Plate 2.3: "Sitka Dock, 1878." M. M. Hazeltine Photo, Oregon Historical Society, #OrHi26958.

30. Plate 2.4: "The *Almota*." Undated. Oregon Historical Society, #OrHi103.

31. Plate 2.5: "Fort Lapwai, Idaho Territory." *New York Daily Graphic*, August 3, 1877. Courtesy of The Chicago Research Library.

32. Plate 2.6: "In Pursuit of Joseph" by Vincent Colyer. *Harper's Weekly*, August 18, 1877. Photo courtesy of Library of Congress.

35. Plate 2.7: "U.S. Troops Crossing Salmon River Rapids." Reproduced by permission of Wood Collection, The Huntington Library, San Marino, California.

36. Plate 2.8: "On Trail Near the Salmon River, July 2, 1877." Guy Howard drawing, Oregon Historical Society, OrHi 102234 #529.

37. Plate 2.9: "Dead Mule Trail, Idaho." Reprinted from *Harper's Weekly*, September 29, 1877. Photo courtesy of Library of Congress.

38. Plate 2.10: "James Reuben, Mark Williams, and Archie B. Lawyer, 1878." Anonymous photo reprinted by permission of Smithsonian Institution, National Anthropological Archives, #2969B.

39.   Plate 2.11: "How the Te-Taw-Ken Came To Be." Reprinted from *A Book of Indian Tales* (New York: Vanguard Press, 1929): 81-83.

41-45. Plates 2.12–2.17: "The Howitzer in a Hot Place," "A Bold Charge on the Right," "Going to the Spring," "Attack on the Pack Train," "The Bivouac," and "Indian Chief." All from *New York Daily Graphic*, August 3, 1877. Courtesy of The Chicago Research Library.

46.   Plate 2.18: "Joseph Red Heart, 1906." Enoch S. Reeves photo courtesy of National Park Service, Nez Perce National Historical Park, Lapwai, Idaho, NEPE–HI–1037.

48.   Plate 2.19: "C.E.S. Wood to Wright P. Edgerton, Camp Cold Springs, Idaho Territory, July 20, 1877." Reprinted courtesy of the Erskine Wood Collection, Aubrey Watzek Library Special Collections, Lewis & Clark College, Portland, Oregon.

50.   Plate 2.20: "Crossing the Clearwater, August, 1877, Nez Perce War." Published courtesy of Yale Collection of Western Americana, Beinecke Rare Book and Manuscript Library, Yale University, #CTYAGC1518-A.

51-54. Plates 2.21–2.23: "A Scout," "Indian Chief [Buffalo Horn], and "An Orphan." All from *New York Daily Graphic*, August 3, 1877. Courtesy of The Chicago Research Library.

PART III. THE ADVOCATE

57-58. Plates 3.1–3.2: "Mountain Passes in the Bitter Root Mountains, " and "Canyons of the Salmon River." *New York Daily Graphic*, August 16, 1877. Courtesy of The Chicago Research Library.

60.   Plate 3.3: "Captives of Joseph's Band Coming Into Miles' Camp." *New York Daily Graphic*, November 3,1877, 1. Courtesy of The Chicago Research Library.

61-62. Plates 3.4–3.5: "A Smohollo, or Medicine Man," and "Camp of Nez Perce on the Clearwater River." *New York Daily Graphic*, August 16, 1877. Courtesy of The Chicago Research Library.

63.   Plate 3.6: "Chief Joseph." *New York Daily Graphic*, November 3, 1877, 1. Courtesy of The Chicago Research Library; quote from Sladen to Lewis Hayden, 20 December, 1877. Howard Papers, Bowdoin College.

65.   Plate 3.7: "A Nez Perce Brave." *New York Daily Graphic*, August 16, 1877. Courtesy of The Chicago Research Library.

74.   Plate 3.8: Letter: Chief Joseph to General O. O. Howard, June 30, 1880. Reprinted courtesy of the Oliver Otis Howard Papers, George J. Mitchell Department of Special Collections & Archives, Bowdoin College Library, Brunswick, Maine.

75. Plate 3.9: General O. O. Howard to Chief Joseph, July 20, 1880. Reprinted courtesy of the Oliver Otis Howard Papers, George J. Mitchell Department of Special Collections & Archives, Bowdoin College Library, Brunswick, Maine.

77. Plate 3.10: "Man's Battle With the Titans Is Begun." *Sonnets*. 1918. Reproduced by permission of Wood Collection, The Huntington Library, San Marino, California. RB 265113.

78. Plate 3.11: "Chief Joseph's Family, Pacific Northwest, ca. 1886." Photographer unknown. Washington State Historical Society, Tacoma, Washington.

PART IV. THE WRITER

81. Plate 4.1: "Wood Family and Friends, Fort Canby, ca. 1888-89." Caption transcribed by Paul Merchant from Erskine Wood notes in 1892 Wood family photo album, page 54. Reprinted courtesy of the Erskine Wood Collection, Aubrey Watzek Library Special Collections, Lewis & Clark College, Portland, Oregon.

84-87. Plates 4.2–4.7: "Wallowa Moraine," "The Receiving Line," "Fulfillment," "Sharon Redthunder with Tom Wood," "Two Gifts," and "The Signing" all published by permission and copyrighted by Suzanne Lewis.

88. Plate 4.8: "Indian Honor Guard Begins the Ceremony , 2000." Photo reprinted courtesy of Fort Vancouver National Historical Site, Washington.

89. Plates 4.9-4.10: "W. Otis Halfmoon, Ft. Vancouver, 1999" and "Empty Saddle Ceremony, Ft. Vancouver, 1999" both reprinted courtesy of the City of Vancouver, Washington.

90. Text: "Reconciliation and Cultural Healing," in "They Did Not Go To War." Donna Sinclair, *Columbia*, Fall, 1998, p. 32. Excerpt reprinted courtesy of the author.

91. Plate 4.11: "Planting the Memorial Grove, 2000." Photo reprinted courtesy of Fort Vancouver National Historic Site, Washington.

Plate 1.1 "Second Lieutenant Charles Erskine Scott Wood, Twenty First Infantry, U.S.Army, 1878."
Taken in Portland, June 6, 1878, the day before he and General Howard boarded the Columbia River steamer *Wide West* for Umatilla, Boise, and the Paiute-Bannock War. This portrait shows Wood's personal evolution from the innocent West Point graduate in 1874, to Gen. Howard's new aide-de-camp in 1877, to the veteran field officer posed here: derringer in hand, pistol on hip, leather cavalry boots, canvas greatcoat, silk scarf, campaign hat, sensitive fearless stare. Concealed inside that coat is his next diary — all blank pages again — along with pens and pencils.

INTRODUCTION

You already know this: the lives of American writers and poets can disappear. In Pacific Northwest literature, first-rate literary biographers are exceptional and few — for some good reasons. Serious biographies themselves are both difficult and exhaustive. Biographers' rewards can be dubious and transient, their typical audience specialized and small. It is no small feat to discover, shape, and publish the story of a writer or poet's life. Fortunately, literary biography is also a cumulative art — each successive biographer hopes to add new information, correct errors, offer interpretations.

So, one purpose of this monograph is biographical: in these pages, I hope to enhance the story of Charles Erskine Scott Wood (1852-1944), the soldier, attorney, writer, best-selling satirist, and artist described by Gordon Dodds as "the only distinguished poet in the Pacific Northwest between 1880 and 1920." To enrich Wood's current portrait, I have transcribed and added historical context to Wood's previously unpublished 1877 originals: diary, letters, and drawings. In all that work, I sensed those originals might best represent Wood, and his character might then be more intelligible to you.

To better contextualize Wood's 1877 experience, I have added photos and drawings by his contemporaries and also quoted excerpts from Wood's published work about the period. Finally, I have integrated the views of historians, principally the stellar work of Jerome Greene and Sherry L. Smith, the latter being the first to distinguish Wood as the "one officer [who] rejected the fundamental assumption of American civilization's superiority." I hope this synthesis will enrich everyone's understanding of Wood's complex character and relationships with Nanny Moale Smith, General Howard, Sitka Jack, a Chilkaht girl, James Reuben (Nez Perce), and Chief Joseph (Nez Perce) — to name a few.

If biographers can keep the lives of American writers and poets from disappearing, who keeps the body of work, the texts and images before readers? Editors, historians, anthologists, teachers, executors, librarians, and archivists share that responsibility. These are not always in short supply, but their roles, access, understanding, and interest may be necessarily limited. In the case of Wood's writing, only one anthology of his work is available, and that collection is not widely known.

So, another purpose of this monograph is textual: to present a sustained look at Wood's prose and poetry about one subject — the 1877 conflict between the non-treaty Nez Perces and the U.S. Army. Fortunately, Wood wrote about that subject throughout his sixty-year career, so in these pages, we can now connect entries in his unpublished soldier's diary to passages in his later poetry. To complement Wood's diverse talent, we can also see — for the first time — twelve drawings he secretly leaked to and published in the New York press — the only eyewitness drawings of the Nez Perce conflict. Finally, from archives across America, I print Wood's unpublished texts grounded in the events of 1877. In juxtaposing all of those originals, I hoped to let Wood's works speak for themselves as much as possible. Taken together, they tell the story of a talented, articulate, young West Point lieutenant who, as a war veteran, never forgot his paradoxical roles: as official staff officer and advocate for his Christian commander Gen. O. O. Howard, and as unofficial sympathizer and advocate for Washani believer Chief Joseph and the non-treaty Nez Perces.

When so many people are responsible for keeping the writer's work current and present, it still falls to literary critics and historians — with an understanding of both Wood's life and writing — to shape the writer's legacy. Among historians, for example, Wood's reputation is divided: he is usually trusted and quoted as a diarist, but usually mistrusted in his account of Chief Joseph's surrender. For over one hundred years, however, editors, anthologists, and critics have published and made famous Wood's heroic sonnet, "The Chief Joseph Surrender Speech." That text — always removed from Wood's legacy of dissent — is still included in national anthologies, textbooks, and histories, and teachers still present it in public schools, colleges, and universities.

Given that dissonance, another purpose of this monograph is thematic: to highlight Wood's legacy of dissent generated by his 1877 Nez Perce conflict experience. Briefly, Wood doubted the Manifest Destiny delusions of his age. He did not believe that Anglo-Americans always represented the good and Nez Perces evil. He did not believe that Anglo-American progress was always superior to Nez Perce tradition. He did not believe that Anglo-American "civilization" must supplant Nez Perce "savagery." While Manifest Destiny advanced the view that the 1877 conflict was caused by forces beyond individual control, Wood asserted that the federal government caused the dispossession, flight, suffering, death, and exile of the non-treaty Nez Perces: the government failed to honor treaties; failed to stop white squatters; failed to trust diplomacy in legal disputes; failed to oppose Nez Perce exile. Wood wrote and/or published all of these criticisms.

In his most imaginative, enduring, and articulate dissent, he did elevate Chief Joseph to the status of a military genius and he did skillfully synthesize Joseph's speech to fit an Anglo-American surrender ceremony and to defend his commander. Years after the surrender, Wood continued to tell the non-treaty Nez Perces' story, to befriend and honor Joseph, and for sixty years Wood's published writing kept the non-treaty bands in the historical record.

To show that Wood's legacy of friendship and respect for the Nez Perces endures, this monograph's last purpose is documentary: to present the Wood family's contemporary efforts to remember and honor the people their literary ancestor Lt. Wood once considered his "enemy," a people he came to respect and admire.

To recognize the Wood family's loyalty, good will, and commitment to justice, I follow their activities with the Nez Perces over the past decade in three different events. In 1991, they participated in the Celebrate Freedom Exhibition titled "C. E. S. Wood and Chief Joseph: Brothers in the American West." In the multi-media program, Wood's grandson read from his grandfather's writing, and a descendent of Chief Joseph read from his 1879 speech. In 1997, the Wood family presented the gift of a stallion to Chief Joseph's descendants in the stolen Wallowa Valley. Since 1998, the Woods have also participated in the Red Heart Memorial Ceremony at Fort Vancouver.

Overall, I hope these multiple and interwoven purposes — biographical, textual, thematic — will enhance everyone's understanding of and appreciation for one American soldier's transformation from soldier to advocate during an unjust war. As presented here, Wood's writing and experience may also address an equally important American malaise — silencing, avoiding, and forgetting what soldiers do and feel and regret and remember, especially soldiers who come to understand and respect their "enemies." To paraphrase James Joyce, Wood shows us all that history is the nightmare from which we should always try to awake.

George Venn

I.

THE EXPLORER: I DO NOT WISH TO LOAF ABOUT SITKA

Close to graduating from the United States Military Academy in spring, 1874, Charles Erskine Scott Wood strongly disliked the idea of becoming an Army officer. The cadet who later became the "one officer [who] rejected the fundamental assumption of American civilization's superiority," the cadet who composed the most controversial text in 19th century western American literature, the cadet who became a Portland lawyer and civic leader — Erskine Wood disliked all that military math and physical science.[1] He disliked military discipline — "work, work, work from reveille to taps" left him no free time for reading novelists and poets. He disliked military routine and piled up "all sorts of petty infractions: inattention at drill, not turning his head and eyes to the left, a soiled collar at guard mounting, shoes not properly blackened at reveille and inspection, swinging his arms as he marched from dinner." He disliked military punishment — being "confined to West Point for six months and forced to stand guard duty every alternate Saturday." He disliked military stoicism — no whistling in the hallways. He disliked being humiliated and hazed and oppressed. Discontent, literate, sociable, imaginative, Erskine wrote his father Dr. Wood that he wanted freedom — to become a writer, or maybe a mercenary, or maybe an orange grower: anyone except a military officer. Every night before bed at West Point, he was secretly writing passionate letters in his new diary for his new love, Nanny Smith.[2]

His father thought Erskine was crazy. Retired Surgeon General of the Navy, Civil War veteran, absentee parent, author, world sailor, Dr. William Maxwell Wood lectured his son: "abandon all feverish and restless desire after change and address yourself with honest and unceasing vigilance to the labor, the claims and obligations of the present around you — and the place and position to which you are called."[3] When his father heard about Erskine's secret lover's diary, he told his son to quit writing such private

---

1. Sherry L. Smith, *The View from Officer's Row* (Tuscon: University of Arizona Press, 1990), 136.

2. Robert Hamburger, *Two Rooms: The Life of Charles Erskine Scott Wood*. (Lincoln: University of Nebraska Press, 1998), 25. This is the only current biography of Wood.

3. Edwin Bingham, *Charles Erskine Scott Wood* (Boise: Boise State University Press, 1990), 11. This monograph is the only contemporary literary study of Wood's writing.

trash. As any son might, Erskine seemed willing to be oppressed by his father's expectations, and in spring, 1874, West Point commissioned him 2nd Lt. Wood — though his dress uniform would conceal Erskine's passion for the freedom to be a writer and artist and his passion to be the lover and husband of Miss Nanny Smith.

On furlough after graduation, the reluctant new lieutenant returned to the idyllic family estate and farm outside Owings Mills, Maryland. During that green and growing summer, Erskine saw his mother Rose Wood, a pious and strict Presbyterian, still struggling to "manage the household and keep up appearances in spite of the damage her husband's spending [and drinking] habits wrought on the family economy." In the home of his innocent childhood, he also saw his retired father, "reduced to alcoholism, bitter and powerless...[,] abuse his mother with ferocious eruptions of temper...." Later, he would say of that summer at Rosewood Glen: "Our home became a wretched place." After courting Nanny all summer, Erskine — at twenty-two — was ripe with passion: he asked permission to marry the "beautiful, histrionic, and coquettish" belle whose "thick chestnut hair came down to her knees," but Miss Smith's stepfather rejected him: new second lieutenants earned a meager $115 per month — barely enough to cover living expenses.[4]

Plate 1.2 "Lt. C. E. S. Wood, West Point Graduation, 1874." Wood "stood apart from his classmates in only two areas: he was one of the top four or five students in drawing [a student of Robert Weir]; and his four-year total of disciplinary demerits was surpassed by only three other cadets" (Hamburger, 30).

Alienated from family, frustrated in love, inspired by the arts, conflicted with militarism, Erskine kissed Nanny Smith farewell, boarded the train in Washington, D.C., and escaped to the mythic west in California. Clattering day and night for three thousand miles on that transcontinental train, he appeared to be a dashing young officer, an innocent with "resolute chiseled features, curly black hair, and keen, penetrating eyes... cultured, self-assured, immensely charming ...[with] high connections and impeccable lineage."[5] As Lt. Wood, he seemed dutiful, obedient,

---

4. Hamburger, 16-31.

5. Hamburger, 9.

official, honorable, but beneath that uniformed military surface, he was also Erskine — the young artist on a private and personal quest for freedom, love, new life, discovery, expression, adventure. As Erskine, he was subversive, mischievous, anarchistic, vulnerable. This division made him human, complex, and potentially literary for, as William Faulkner said, "the problems of the human heart in conflict with itself... alone can make good writing...."[6]

When he arrived at Camp Bidwell, his assigned Army post in northern California, a love letter from Nanny Smith was waiting for him. "Of course, that letter made me very happy," he would say years later.[7] As Nanny's impecunious lover, Erskine wrote regularly to her — the "most sought-after belle in Washington, D.C."[8] Ignoring his father's attempt to quash a young writer's dreams, Erskine wrote and mailed "a manuscript to his brother Maxwell at the Navy

Plate 1.3 "Miss Nanny Moale Smith, 1872." Petite, histrionic, sociable, Nanny and Wood met and fell in love when she was seventeen — the summer this photo was taken. The day Wood graduated from West Point, Nanny did not attend. She was 'flirting desperately' with Tracy Gould, [and] "chose to stay in Troy [New York] with her new love interest... Wood was crushed..." To overcome his fear of losing her before he left for the west, they met again in Washington. "Without a formal engagement but with a clear understanding that they would remain true to each other and eventually marry, they parted" (Philip Leon, *Nanny Wood*, 43).

department in Washington, D.C., requesting that Max try to place it with *Harpers* or *Scribners*." When Max reported that Erskine's manuscript had been rejected for "being 'too deep for the reading public,'" he also "encouraged his younger brother to turn to lighter, more attractive subjects growing out of experiences and materials close

---

6. William Faulkner, "Speech of Acceptance upon the award of the Nobel Prize for Literature," in *The Faulkner Reader* (New York: Random House, 1943), 3.

7. Carton 28, Cylinder A-1 Transcript, 2, C. E. S. Wood Collection, Huntington Library, San Marino, California [hereafter Wood Collection].

8. Hamburger, 1.

at hand...[such as] little sketches... of some of the *funnier ports*..., [with] a little mirth, a little love, and a good deal of fiction.... Do this. Don't write trash. Cultivate a style of your own — concise free and simple....'"[9]

Now, three thousand miles from West Point, the Lt. Wood who disliked militarism did his duty: "I took my company allotment of recruits and drilled them into shape and my captain [Robert Pollock] said he wouldn't want anything better than that...and that's about all they gave me to do...." For Capt. Pollock, the new lieutenant also "took over the company's record keeping and report writing," a duty which allowed him some freedom to write and explore and map the surrounding country, and to meet and camp and live with a Paiute Indian family.[10] Off duty, Erskine recalled that he "commenced to look

Plate 1.4 "Lieutenant C.E.S. Wood, Fort Vancouver, Washington Territory, January 1, 1877." After six years of courtship, coast-to-coast love letters, brief visits, discussions, on-and-off engagement, and disquieted families, Wood and Nanny were married in Baltimore on November 26, 1878, "and departed on the midnight train for an odd honeymoon" — a transcontinental train ride to California, then steam ship to Portland (Leon, 59).

around to amuse myself — the bird life, the animal life and the rancher's life.... I didn't play cards... [T]here were occasional balls...and I invariably went to them because at West Point I had been a good dancer...The ranch young women were very good looking and there wasn't much else to do...we were practically imprisoned up there...."[11]

By August, 1875, these multiple personae and their conflicting commitments — military, literary, and romantic — had not changed. When Lt. Wood's company was transferred to Fort Vancouver in Washington Territory, he marched these complex

---

9. Bingham, *Charles Erskine Scott Wood*, 12.

10. Wood's commanding officer is Capt. Robert Pollock, Twenty-first Infantry. Hamburger, 6. For further references to Pollock, see diary entries in Part II. For insight and comment on living with the Paiutes, see Sherry L. Smith, *Reimagining Indians* (Oxford University Press, 2000), 21-44.

11. Diaries (1913-1924), Carton 28, Cylinder A-1 Transcript, 1-2, Wood Collection.

personae across the Great Basin — from Fort Bidwell to The Dalles. En route, he filled a personal diary with his delight at the wild world of waterbirds and rimrock and sage, the beauty of high desert stars and coyotes and owls, the wonders of the Malheur oasis, Blitzen River, Alvord Desert, upthrust Steens. Years later, Erskine's most private and important poems and paintings would arise from this remote Oregon region, and eventually he would be described as "the only distinguished poet" in the Pacific Northwest between 1880 and 1920.[12]

Early in the winter of 1876, his commanding officer at Fort Vancouver sent Lt. Wood to Army headquarters in Portland, a mission that would permanently change his life. As he later recalled,

Plate 1.5 "Mrs. Nanny Smith Wood, Portland, 1879." Active and gracious mother of five, Nanny endured Wood's numerous affairs, and when her estranged husband left her for the poet Sara Bard Field, Nanny refused divorce for fifteen years. "Though Nannie's anguish and injured pride never passed, her Portland life remained richly satisfying until age and illness claimed her" (Hamburger, *Two Rooms*, 323).

"The Columbia was full of running ice and no one would take me across... finally I found a flat bottom skiff — appropriated it and set out pushing my way through the ice as openings came and of course going slowly down with the current.... Just before I got even with... Hayden Island I found the seams of my boat had been plugged with ice frozen in them which had now melted. The skiff was filling with water and I hardly got to where I could get ashore when she sank. I let her go, walked across the island — only a couple of hundred yards or so — then... some wood choppers got me across to the mainland... then I walked a muddy road through dense fir forest... and delivered my dispatches to Gen. Howard. I rather think that was our first meeting. Anyway he took a fancy to me...."[13]

The General's "fancy" was both personal and military. Both Brig. Gen. Oliver O. Howard and his wife, Elizabeth Howard, welcomed the sociable and handsome young man as a family member. At the Howard home — the present Tenth and Morrison in Portland — Erskine would frequently take his meals, stay overnight, and visit with the general, Mrs. Howard, the young Howard children, and "Howard's daughter Grace [who] had recently graduated from Vassar College and found her father's post grievously lacking in suitable companions."[14] In 1879, when the Howards moved to their new home at Fort Vancouver, they provided Erskine with a room of his own.[15] In

---

12. Gordon Dodds, *The American Northwest* (Arlington Heights, Ill: Forum Press, 1986), 159; Charles Erskine Scott Wood, *The Poet in the Desert* (New York: Vanguard, 1929). See Bingham, *Charles Erskine Scott Wood*, 13-14, for extensive use of Wood's unpublished journal from this march.

13. "Wood Diary," WD Box 29(4), July 10, 1928, Wood Collection.

14. Hamburger, *Two Rooms*, 33.

15. Doug Halsey, National Park Service, Fort Vancouver, Wash., interview by author, August 29, 2001.

a letter to Howard some eight years later, Erskine summarized the evolution of their relationship: "I came to you a boy, I lived at your house, loved your family. Mrs. Howard was a mother to me. I loved Grace as my own sister... I married from your house, you stood sponsor for our first home, my father died and I felt the sympathy of all of you."[16]

In Gen. Howard, Erskine found not only a benign father but also a supportive literary mentor. To supplement his Army income, Howard was already publishing in religious papers and eastern magazines. So, when the young writer could not cross the icy Columbia, he and the general began corresponding about writing — a commonplace in literary life. On January 11, 1876, for instance, Erskine sent Howard a manuscript with the following note: "I ought to mention that I made no attempt at any broad humor or burlesque except twice and I tried to cover under a smile many points that are worth while thinking of seriously; for I wouldn't waste my time in trying to make people smile and *only* smile." In another letter to the general he wrote, "Here's a description of the detail of a battle. A sort of microscopical view in which the minutiae are made visible to the exclusion of the vast and important objects. It may possibly be of some service to you tho' I think not. I would like to have it again if you will kindly keep it for me." Two weeks later, Gen. Howard responded: "Dear Wood: I send back these slips. The writer gives graphic incidents. I do not forget scenes as trying & exciting & plaintive... Yours gratefully, O. O. Howard."[17] In their

Plate 1.6 "Gen. O. O. Howard." Described in the New York *Daily Graphic* as "a recent photograph by Buchtel & Slote [sic] of Portland, Oregon," this engraving of a studio portrait shows the commanding officer and friend who privileged Wood with the opportunity to explore Alaska. Published August 3, 1877, under the headline, "General Howard's Battle With the Nez Perces Indians, July 11," the photo gave official credibility to Wood's ten sketches attributed to "an Officer of General Howard's Staff." (See Part II.) That anonymity protected Wood from potential censure for leaking information directly to the press — a violation of Army policy.

---

16. C. E. S. Wood to Gen. Howard, March 19, 1883. Oliver Otis Howard Papers, Bowdoin College Library, Brunswick, Maine [hereafter Howard Papers].

17. Wood to Howard, January 11, 1876, March 1, 1876. Howard Papers. For Wood's later satires attacking orthodox conservatism — "patriotism, prudery, bigotry, censorship, dogmatic Christianity, and organized religion," — see one of his most famous works, *Heavenly Discourse* (New York: Vanguard Press, 1927); Edwin Bingham and Tim Barnes, eds, *Wood Works* (Corvallis: Oregon State University Press, 1997), 265-88.

literary correspondence, Howard's notorious religiosity apparently did not surface. If confronted with the "Christian General's" fundamentalism, however, Wood could readily understand — or dissemble. As a child, he had been raised in a strict religious family, so strict, in fact, that Erskine "loathed and hated Sundays."[18] Simultaneous with these literary exchanges, "Erskine wrote regularly to Nanny — lengthy letters, almost comically conventional, gushing with the ardent spirit of young love."[19]

In addition to this personal and private writing, Lt. Wood took up an official military role as Howard's judge advocate, a roaming and privileged position that required Lt. Wood to settle and write up "legal and jurisdictional disputes as well as questions involving military discipline and criminal acts" throughout the Department of the Columbia.[20] As Erskine later explained, he was "ordered around rather promiscuously[:] to Puget Sound...in a rather important case...[;] to the mouth of the Columbia to attend to some matters of government rights...[;] to Fort Walla Walla to get material for confidential reports." All this region-wide travel and work as judge advocate "gave [him] a black eye in the regiment," so he asked Capt. Pollock to "find some real company or regimental duties." When Gen. Howard received this request, he refused to reassign his favored and literary lieutenant who was "doing him and the government more service in faithfully administering those [judge advocate] offices and duties...[than those] he [Pollock] allotted me."[21]

By April, 1877, Lt. Wood was well-known to Gen. Howard. When addressing him, he always used the familiar "Wood." One surprising spring day, Howard wrote a note and sent it across the Columbia to Vancouver Barracks:

> Headquarters Department of the Columbia
> Portland, OGN, April 5, 1877
>
> Dear Wood,
>   If you would like to go with Mr. C. K. Taylor Scientist on a trip to Alaska starting Saturday morning from Portland, come on with such hasty preparation as you can make by the Vancouver [boat] tomorrow (Friday) — or by the Dalles boat Friday evening. You would probably be gone two months. Ask Capt Miles to assign one of his lieutenants to your company.
>
>   Yours truly
>   O. O. Howard
>   Brig. Gen. U.S.A.
>   Comdg. Dept.[22]

---

18. Hamburger, *Two Rooms*, 16.

19. Ibid., 33.

20. Ibid, 35.

21. Carton 21, Wax Cylinder Transcript, 1, Wood Collection.

22. Howard to Wood. Courtesy of the Erskine Wood Collection, Aubrey Watzek Library Special Collections, Lewis & Clark College, Portland, Oregon. Transcribed by Paul Merchant.

Plate 1.7 "Taylor Expedition in Sitka." Taken in late April, 1877, by an unknown photographer, Wood (*third from left*) named almost everyone: "We finally closed a bargain with Tah-ah-han-klekh [*far left*] for his canoe of about four tons burden. He was to act as pilot and steersman. We hired Nach-sach, Klen, and Jack as crew.... [Louis] Myers went with us as prospector and miner" (*Century* XXIV, 325).

As freedom-seeking Erskine later explained, "In 24 hours I was on the [steamer] *California* bound for Sitka."[23] Heading north to explore wild Alaska, Lt. Wood carried a thin brown leather-bound 5" x 8" vest pocket notebook — thirty unnumbered lined blank pages ready to be filled by the exploring mind — a commonplace for beginning writers. Erskine probably intended to use this private "diary of situation" as a literary "source book that might be mined for materials to be used in [later]... public writing —" poem, article, essay, autobiography.[24]

After five weeks escorting Charles Taylor's expedition (not recorded in this diary) Lt. Wood returned to rainy Sitka, and Charles Taylor sailed for Portland. Waiting out a three-day rain storm in sodden Sitka, Erskine sat down — probably at Army headquarters — to write his friend and commander:

---

23. "Wood Diary," WD Box 29(4), July 10, 1928. Wood Collection.

24. Steven E. Kagle, *American Diary Literature: 1620-1799* (Boston: Twayne, 1979), 142; Steven E. Kagle, *Early Nineteenth Century Diary Literature* (Boston: Twayne, 1986), 104.

Sitka Alaska, May 16, 1877

My Dear General,

    I want to give you a hasty sketch of my doings so that you may reflect whether to give your approval or disapproval of them. Mr. Taylor and I left here on the 24th of last month and taking the inside passage through Peril Straits to Chatam Strait, and up these latter Straits to Cross Sound, we proceeded in one of the medium sized canoes, in charge of four Indians, as far as the inner bay of Cape Spencer; and there the Indians made a stand and refused to go farther, saying no canoe could live in the open sea through a voyage of five or seven days; that no canoe ever had done it and plainly intimating that that particular canoe never would. The passage to this point had been inside the straits and narrows of the archipelago and was as safe as river travel. The Indians had come this far with us owing to a misunderstanding; believing that Mt. Fairweather was the "Big Mountain" we wished to climb and the "Yakitat" Bay we had spoken of was the bay running close in to this mountain.

    Mr. Taylor finding we could go no further turned immediately and we raced to catch the May steamer, which we did, arriving on the same day as she — the 9th inst [present month].

    Owing to our hasty travel both ways I could see nothing and do nothing and upon my second arrival at this place Sitka Jack having returned (He and Skineah were absent at the time I left.) I went to see him and ask if I could get up the Chilcat river into the interior of the country. He said in substance that the Chilcat chief, his brother-in-law, had received a visit from General Howard the one armed Big Tyhee who had promised two years ago to send an officer to see him and that the Chilcat chief wanted to see an officer, that he would give him boys and send him up the river, that he (the Chief) wanted his country explored, wanted the mines opened, wanted maps made and would help any one to do this who did not trade nor shoot his game and fur animals, that the Chief would like to see me.

    Mr. Phillipson says his schooner will return about the 15th of June and that he is going to trade with the Chilcat chief at his village and that he will take me along and turn me over to the chief and talk to him for me and maybe go up the river with me. In any case if this barbarian Chilcat monarch will send me up the river I would like very much to go. I will map his country for him roughly with compass notes — it is the only instrument I have — and I will take Louis Myers the Vancouver prospector who came up with us and have him explore the minerals.

    He, Myers, was with Mr. Taylor and found lead with silver at our last camp, but we left the same day so he had no time to investigate. He wished very much to return to that section as it seemed to be of good mineral character in all its general appearances and the Indians told great yarns of coal, silver, lead, copper, etc, so on the permission you gave me to stay behind Mr. Taylor to collect any information of value or complete any notes on the country, hearing nothing new from Wallowa or Vancouver I have taken the liberty of staying even a steamer to hear from you about my going to the Chilcat country and as I do not wish to loaf about Sitka I have fitted out a small expedition of my own to take Myers and go up to Cape Spencer and around Mt. Fairweather and take a look at the country, its resources and inhabitants. Really there is nothing known of this country, the ignorance of the traders and store-keepers who live here is simply gross and marvellous [sic]. They can tell you nothing or if they do venture on a bit of information and you follow it up it is sure to be found false. I have no hesitation in pronouncing my trip a perfectly safe one. I would do nothing rash nor anything to annoy you but I have carefully considered it, have asked advice upon it and have already been once in the same country and I know there is no more danger than there is right in Vancouver. You know the Indians and know also that the route is all inland and I think you will agree with me. I would like to do a little something before I come down. There will be three whites of us and two Indians. I have put all my money in it because the Chilcat trip will cost me little or nothing.

> Phillipson will take me up and bring me back free of charge and if the Chilcat chief will not send me up in royal state in dead-head canoe I will not go, or at most only go a day or two up the river.
>
> I shall use every effort to return from the Cape Spencer country in time for the June steamer so I can return on that if your judgement is against sending me to the Chilcat chief, but, subject always to your wishes in the matter, I should like very much to go. I will be prudent and I think I can return on the July steamer.
>
> I wish it were only possible that I could get some orders to give me all summer up in the Chilcat country so that I could explore the headwaters of the Yukon.
>
> Maj. Canby and his party are here but it has been wet and disagree-able weather. In fact, I am storm bound and have been ready for the past three days to leave the instant the weather changes. Canby tells me that Poor Knapp is dead, it is very sad, a peculiarly sad death, I think; and he says too that Smith of the 21st killed himself. This brings Boyle the Captaincy for which he has so patiently waited. Please to tell him that I am glad he has searched such a good resting place as now-a-days a captaincy is. Will you remember me kindly to Wilkinson and the other officers as you may see them, not forgetting Gen. Eaton and Babbitt. I will keep what else I have to tell you, for another time. I have written in great haste but this letter is much too long. I am
>
> Very sincerely your friend,
>
> C. E. S. Wood[25]

Without waiting for Howard's reply, Erskine formed his own canoe crew and left Sitka, as he wrote four years later, "to explore the bay [Glacier Bay], cross the coast range, and strike the upper waters of the Chilkaht [River]." For several weeks, he and his party engaged the wild beauty of Alaskan landscape and Tlingit culture. As with the Paiute family in California, Erskine again sought authentic cross-cultural experience and understanding. He traveled and ate and slept among friendly Asonque villagers. He studied and interviewed them and they observed and questioned him. He sketched their artifacts, observed their customs, wrote down their stories, and relished their rich and ancient traditions — feasts, shamans, totems, ceremonies, masks, salmon, hunts, canoes, seals. Describing his return to Sitka, Erskine wrote about stopping at a Hoonah camp on Cross Sound where he doctored various patients, exchanged stories, feasted, drew pictures, exchanged gifts, and for his services, the old Hoonah chief offered him "a wife from among the women of his household" — probably chosen from the "youngest and prettiest" who sat on both sides of him. In 1882, when Erskine's Alaska article — a mix of autobiography, ethnography, and poetry — appeared in *Century Magazine*, he alluded to but did not disclose this sexual favor — though years later, he confessed that erotic night to a friend.[26] Like Lewis and Clark and many other explorers before him, Erskine censored himself when writing about sexual experience with Native American women. When publishing his first article in America's most prestigious monthly, he could not risk candor. A recent historian has even claimed that such "a public acknowledgment of this sexual relationship with an Indian woman would have obviated any possibility of marriage to Nanny; moreover, his army career would have

---

25. C. E. S. Wood to Gen. Howard, May 16, 1877. Howard Papers.

26. "Among the Thlinkits in Alaska." *Century Monthly XXIV* (July 1882):323-39, reprinted in *Wood Works*, Bingham and Barnes,eds., 43-63. For the sexual favor admitted years later, see Smith, *Reimagining Indians*, 23-26.

Plate 1.8 "The Indian Village at Sitka." Signed by H. Bolton Jones, this sketch illustrated Wood's 1882 *Century* article. Because Jones never traveled to Alaska, he may have used a Wood pencil sketch or adapted this from an unsigned 1879 engraving in William Morris and James Swan's *Report upon the customs district, public service, and resources of Alaska Territory*. Writing later, Wood recalled, "The Indian village is built upon the beach, and at evening it was covered by the shadow of the adjoining forest" (*Century* XXIV, 1882, 324).

Plate 1.9 "Yakutat Natives in Potlatch Dancing Costumes. Sitka, Alaska... c. 1904." In May, 1877, Wood met "Sitka Jack" — here kneeling and holding a ceremonial pole. Wood later described Jack as "an arrant old scoundrel, but one of the wealthiest men of the Sitka tribe. Of course, his house stood among the largest, at the fashionable end of town" (*Century* XXIV, 325).

been effectively ended."[27]

Returning to Sitka in early June, Lt. Wood "received word that the army had granted him the three-year leave he requested... [but] he also learned that "the Nez Perce Indians had attacked settlers... [and] his Twenty-first Regiment had been called to the front."[28] To further complicate Erskine's quest for freedom and adventure, he was out of money and all his fellow soldiers were withdrawing from Sitka. Now, he had to choose: Should he stay in the north alone and dare more unfunded exploring? Should he go south with his comrades on the monthly steamer? By June 11, he decided: though Erskine had just enjoyed the freedom of a cross-cultural adventure among the Tlingit, as Lt. Wood he now conformed, fell in, and sailed south for trouble.

Plate 1.10 "Thlinkit Woman (Sitka Kwahn)." Based on an unknown photograph, this Alfred Brennan sketch may have been commissioned to illustrate Wood's visit with the old Hoonah chief: "At his bountiful board I had a seat between his youngest and prettiest wives. They prepared seal-flipper for me with a celery-like dressing of some plant. We lived in ease and luxury with a little necessary grease and dirt" (*Century* XXIV, 1882, 338).

How much Lt. Wood knew about the causes of the Nez Perce-U.S. Army conflict when he boarded that steamer to leave Alaska on June 11, 1877, is an open question. If he had read Colonel Clay Wood's 1875-76 report, *Status of Young Joseph and His Band of Nez Perce Indians...*, he might well have been disturbed. It was widely known that, "because Joseph's band had never signed the 1863 agreement [treaty,] ... the band could not be forced to move... [and that] Howard was so impressed... he wrote to the War Department, 'I think it a great mistake to take from Joseph and his band of Nez Perces Indians that valley [the Wallowa].'"[29]

Since saving the lives of the Lewis and Clark expedition in 1805, the Nez Perces had maintained peaceful and friendly relations for more than sixty years with fur trappers, white missionaries, soldiers, and government agents, and in 1855 they signed a treaty with the United States that apportioned 6.4 million acres to the five Nez Perce

---

27. Philip W. Leon, *Nanny Wood: From Washington Belle to Portland's Grande Dame* (Bowie, Maryland: Heritage Books, 2003), 61.

28. Hamburger, *Two Rooms*, 41.

29. Bruce Hampton, *Children of Grace* (New York: Henry Holt, 1994) 42; Major Henry Clay Wood, *Status of Young Joseph and His Band of Nez Perce Indians...* (Portland: Ore.: Assistant Adjutant General's Office of Headquarters Department of Columbia, 1876).

THE SONG OF THE SALMON FISHING

Why is the young man sorrowful?
Oh why is the young man sad?
Ah-ka. His maiden has left him.
The long suns have come,
The ice now is melting;
Now comes the salmon
He leaps in the river,
In the moon's gentle twilight
He throws up a bow–
A bow of bright silver.
Lusty and strong he darts through the water,
He sports with his mate;
He springs from the water.
All the dark season
He has lain hidden.
Now he comes rushing,
And ripples the river.
Purple and gold, and red and bright silver
Shine on his sides and flash in his sporting,
How he thrashes the net!
How he wrenches the spear!
But the red of his sides
Is stained with a redder;
The maid of the young man leans o'er the salmon
White laugh her teeth,
Clear rings her laughter;
Which passes canoes all busy and happy,
Which outstrips the noise of the many mixed voices
And pierces the heart of her sorrowful lover.
She has forgot him,
She joys with another.
All for another she chases the salmon,
Ah-ka. Your sweetheart has left you.
So do they jeer him,
Ah-ka — your sweetheart is here at the fishing!
Ah-ka — how like you this gay salmon season?

Plate 1.11 "Song of the Salmon Fishing." Masking his first published poem as a translation, Wood attributes this love lyric to a "niece of the Chilkaht chief, one of the comeliest of her race, who had married a hideously ugly, but very rich old Hoonah.... [She] mended my clothes and my sealskin boots and sang sad songs or chants for my entertainment that were quite wonderful...for their flowing measure and rhythm. This is one which I learned to understand the best..." (*Century* XXIV, 338).

bands living in Oregon, Washington, and Idaho. In 1863, the federal government wanted to negotiate a new treaty that would reduce the 1855 Nez Perce lands to 784,996 acres in Idaho alone — about one tenth of their former holdings. During those negotiations, Lawyer, the head chief of the treaty faction, was misled by white officials and arrogated to himself, "the right and obligation to speak for all the bands and to sign away all the lands of Joseph, White Bird, and every other Nez Perce...who lived outside the [Idaho] reservation. Lawyer... neither objected to that act nor explained that he did not possess the right to do what he had done."[30] The government agent who negotiated that 1863 treaty "secured the signature or the agreement of every headman whose lands the new treaty

Plate 1.12 "The Main Street of Sitka." Signed H. Bolton Jones. Since Jones himself had never seen Sitka, Wood may have provided him with his own rough pencil sketch. Perhaps Jones could then illustrate the following passage in Wood's 1882 *Century* article. "The green spire on the belfry of the Greek church reached up above everything... The church on the lower ground was surrounded by the rambling dilapidated houses and hovels of the Russian inhabitants, who then numbered about four hundred..." (*Century* XXIV, 1882, 324).

would not affect, *but did not secure the signatures of Joseph, White Bird, or any leader, save Timothy and Jason, who lived outside the borders of the new reservation*" [emphasis added]. By the new treaty's terms, all of the [non-treaty] bands were required to move on the reservation [in Idaho] within one year after the document was ratified."[31] Erskine would have known that Joseph and his Wallowa Valley band had not signed the 1863 treaty, that they and other non-treaty bands rightfully refused to leave homelands legally agreed to be theirs in 1855. As Howard's roaming judge advocate, he may also have known about the failures of various commissions and councils to right the obvious injustices — murder, rape, trespass, and theft — committed against the non-treaty bands by invading white settlers, miners, and headmen of the Christianized treaty bands.

---

30. Alvin Josephy, *Nez Perce Country: A Handbook for Nez Perce National Historical Park, Idaho* (Washington, D.C., U.S. Department of the Interior, 1983), 106-112.

31. Alvin Josephy, *The Nez Perce Indians and the Opening of the Pacific Northwest* (New Haven: Yale University Press, 1965), 386-442.

Plate 1.13 "Interior of Chief Klart-Reech's House, Chilkat, Alaska." ca. 1895 During 1877, Wood visited five chiefs' houses: Sitka Jack, Jack's brother-in-law, Chief Cocheen, an Asonque chief, an old Hoonah chief. Writing later about his Tlingit experience, Wood suggests he witnessed scenes similar to this — dancers on a platform in the Whale House. Here, eleven men and boys dress in old costumes with two bentwood boxes, a wormwood dish, rainwall screen, house posts of Raven and the Girl, and the carved woodwork background.

Plate 1.14 "U.S. Army Headquarters, Sitka, Alaska." ca. 1868-69 During April and May, 1877, Wood likely walked the dirt street to this building where he sat out the rain, wrote to Gen. Howard, took diary notes on the talk of fellow officers, and — as recorded in his diary — helped round up drunk soldiers.

Lt. Wood could not have known, however, the chief reason his Twenty-first Infantry battalion had now been called to "war." When the Lapwai Council concluded on May 15, Erskine had been exploring Alaska and learning Tlingit culture. No telegram, letter, or messenger from Fort Lapwai could have reached him with the ominous news: Gen. Howard had turned the peaceful Lapwai council from a legitimate treaty rights forum into a bellicose, ethnocentric, and racist assault. Failing to grant the validity of non-treaty rights, becoming intolerant of cultural and religious differences, trusting force to intimidate the parties in a legal dispute, and knowing he had the approval of racist Indian agents, settlers, state and federal agencies, Gen. Howard had imprisoned Toohoolhoolzote, the chief Nez Perce orator, and proclaimed his militarist ultimatum: all non-treaty Nez Perces had thirty days to "remove" from their legally-held homelands

Plate 1.15 "Chief Lawyer." ca. 1861 James Lawyer (*Hallalhotsoot*) was a friend of the missionaries and head chief of the treaty faction of the tribe. Misled by white officials, Lawyer signed away 5.6 million acres of non-treaty Nez Perce lands in 1863. He died at Kamiah on January 3, 1876, and was buried in the cemetery of the Presbyterian church.

or face the threat of "removal" by his forces. Wanting to avoid the bloodshed Howard threatened, the Wallowa band had, in fact, crossed the Snake River and were moving to the Idaho reservation when four young men from White Bird's band — shamed by years of white greed, invasion, murder, and theft — retaliated against settlers along the Salmon River. In the U. S. military imagination, this retribution became "the outbreak of war." Reimagining the tribe that saved the lives of Lewis and Clark as "the enemy," Gen. Howard then ordered around a hundred cavalry to attack "the hostiles" camped on White Bird Creek. In that battle, Nez Perce warriors — outnumbered two to one

Plate 1.16 "Chief Joseph's Band, Lapwai, Idaho, Spring, 1877." In Alaska at this time, Wood later researched, then wrote about these mounted non-treaty Nez Perces and their leaders — Joseph, White Bird, and Looking Glass: "They came singing the monotonous chants of the wilderness, with gaudy blankets flaunting in the wind or girded at the loins. The horses were daubed with color and plumed with eagle feathers. As they galloped and curveted, the fantastic head-dresses, crests, and flowing locks of their riders, the red leggings or bare brown legs, arms, and breasts, the eagle-feather and bear-claw trimmings, made a highly colored and animated picture" (*Century* XXVIII, 1884, 136).

— killed thirty-four men and forced the survivors to panic and retreat.[32]

Sailing down the rainy Inside Passage the afternoon of June 17, Lt. Wood had no idea that ten days later, the hot afternoon of June 27, he would help bury those first soldiers killed at White Bird, and record his first five weeks as an infantry officer in his diary transcribed in Part II. He could not have known that, after fifteen days of marching mostly in a circle, Gen. Howard would promote him to aide-de-camp, then ask him — confidentially — to defend the general's national reputation by drawing sketches and writing stories and leaking both to the New York press. Erskine could never have imagined that for the next four months — actually, for the rest of his life — he would play a part in what historians generally agree was the "meanest, most contemptible, least justifiable thing that the United States was ever guilty of " — the U.S. Army's eviction and seventeen-hundred-mile pursuit of around eight hundred fleeing and fighting non-treaty Nez Perce men, women, and children with their baggage and horse herd.[33]

---

32. See the literature cited throughout these notes for some of the many accounts of this conflict, most recently the work of Jerome Greene, who takes up one key disputed issue here: what terms should be used to accurately portray and interpret these events? Was this a "war," or a "conflict?" Jerome Greene, *Nez Perce Summer 1877* (Helena: Montana Historical Society Press, 2000, xiv). Another historian correctly explains that American military terms, such as "war," "retreat," and "surrender" could be applied to Gen. Howard's actions, but those terms "have all too frequently presented a military picture which distorts Indian operations during that conflict." See Merle Wells, "The Nez Perce and Their War." *Pacific Northwest Quarterly 55*, 1 (January, 1964): 35-37. Note: Wells himself inadvertently resorts to military terms, fails to note that the non-treaty Nez Perce are, in fact, refugees, and does not state that Howard's wielding of military terms converted a legitimate legal dispute over treaty rights into a "war."

33. J. P. Dunn, *Massacres of the Mountains: A History of the Indian Wars of the Far West* (New York: Harper, 1886. Rpt. Capricorn Books, 1969), 527.

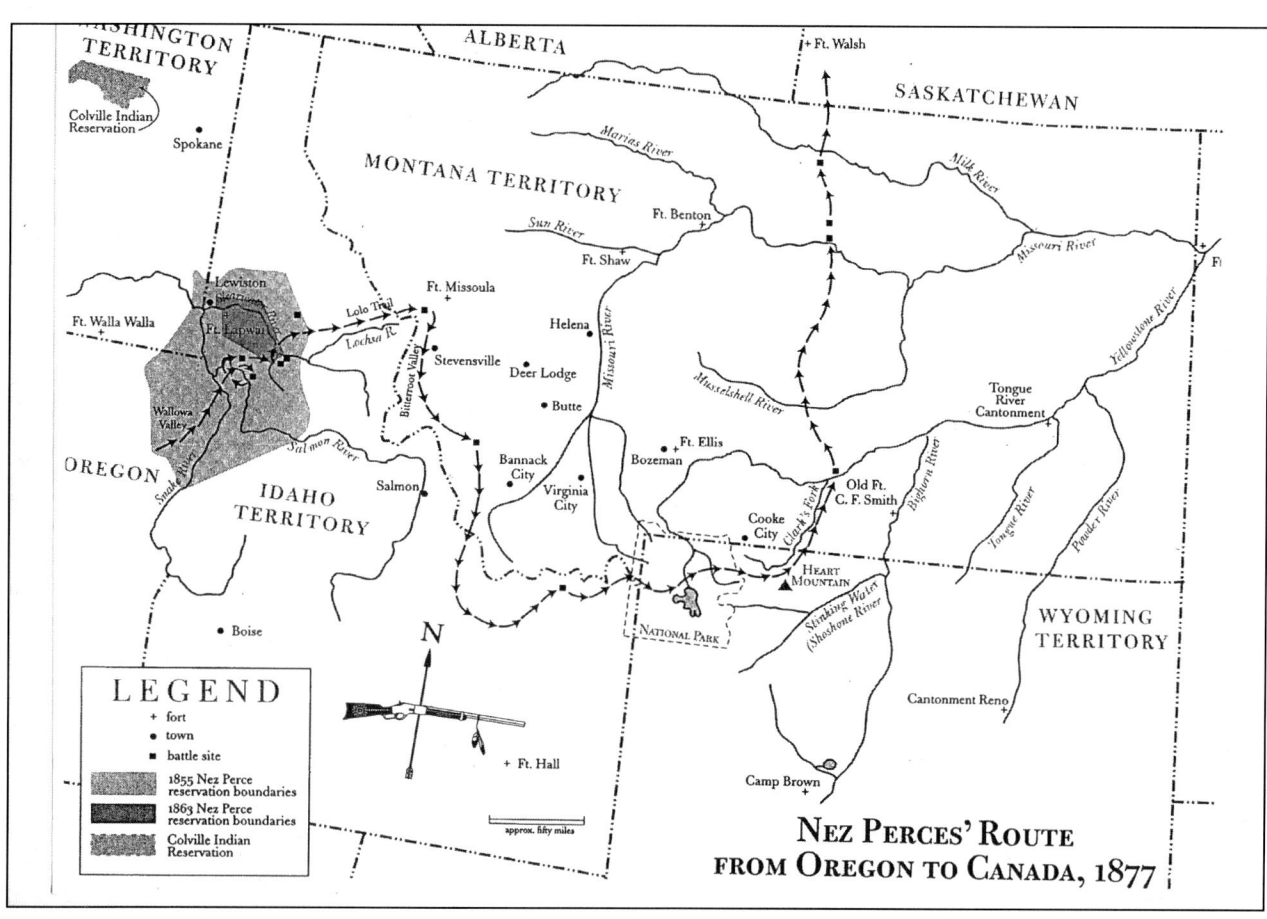

Plate 1.17 "Nez Perces' Route from Oregon to Canada, 1877." The loss of 5.6 million acres of non-treaty bands' homeland, as shown here, was negotiated in 1863 by Chief Lawyer, a treaty band leader on the Lapwai reservation. In central Idaho, Wood marched for five weeks as an infantry lieutenant, then became Gen. Howard's aide-de-camp on July 22. For the next three months, Wood traversed the same general route shown here for the fleeing Nez Perces. Jerome Greene, *Nez Perce Summer 1877* (Helena: Montana Historical Society Press, 2000: 9).

II.

THE SOLDIER'S DIARY:
FACING THE PROBABILITIES BY WRITING

One of Wood's few surviving original texts from that summer of 1877, the diary transcribed in the following pages has two distinct sections: Part 1 is Alaska entries written between April 14 and June 17, 1877, and confirmed by Erskine himself as incomplete: "When I set out to explore Alaska, I began a journal and kept it faithfully for three days while I was on the steamer."[1] Wood's most recent biographer notes that "[These] fragments... from his Sitka journal suggest that he [Wood] wished to produce a humorous anecdotal account of frontier life, its roguish characters, and colorful speech" in the manner of Bret Harte and Mark Twain.[2] They may also reflect his brother Max's advice cited earlier: write "little sketches... of some of the *funnier ports*..., [with] a little mirth, a little love, and a good deal of fiction." Part 2 of Wood's diary records his first five weeks in the U.S. Army-Nez Perce conflict in Oregon and Idaho — entries written between June 19 and July 23, 1877. Like the first section from Alaska exploration, this section is also incomplete. Another commonplace of young writers called to adventure appears: the novice buys a blank diary, starts to write daily entries, but life — action, excitement, exhaustion, weather — takes over. Art disappears. Blank pages march on and on. Erskine did not intend this text as a complete, official, or exact historical record. In fact, he argued against making "history from the diaries of soldiers."[3]

In the second section cited by numerous historians and Wood's biographer, readers can engage the rough notes of a young and undifferentiated writer in his multiplicity of conflicted personae. As Erskine, he cryptically and tacitly records his initiation by conflict and complexity into racism, injustice, militarism, identity — some of the same forces he first encountered as a West Point cadet. In these pages, he also faces unknowns

---

1. Autobiographical Notes, Wood Collection, WD Box 6 (7).

2. Robert Hamburger, *Two Rooms: The Life of Charles Erskine Scott Wood* (Lincoln: University of Nebraska Press, 1998), 37.

3. C. E. S Wood to McWhorter, March 12, 1941, cited in *Hear Me, My Chiefs* (Caldwell, Idaho: Caxtons, 1952), 260.

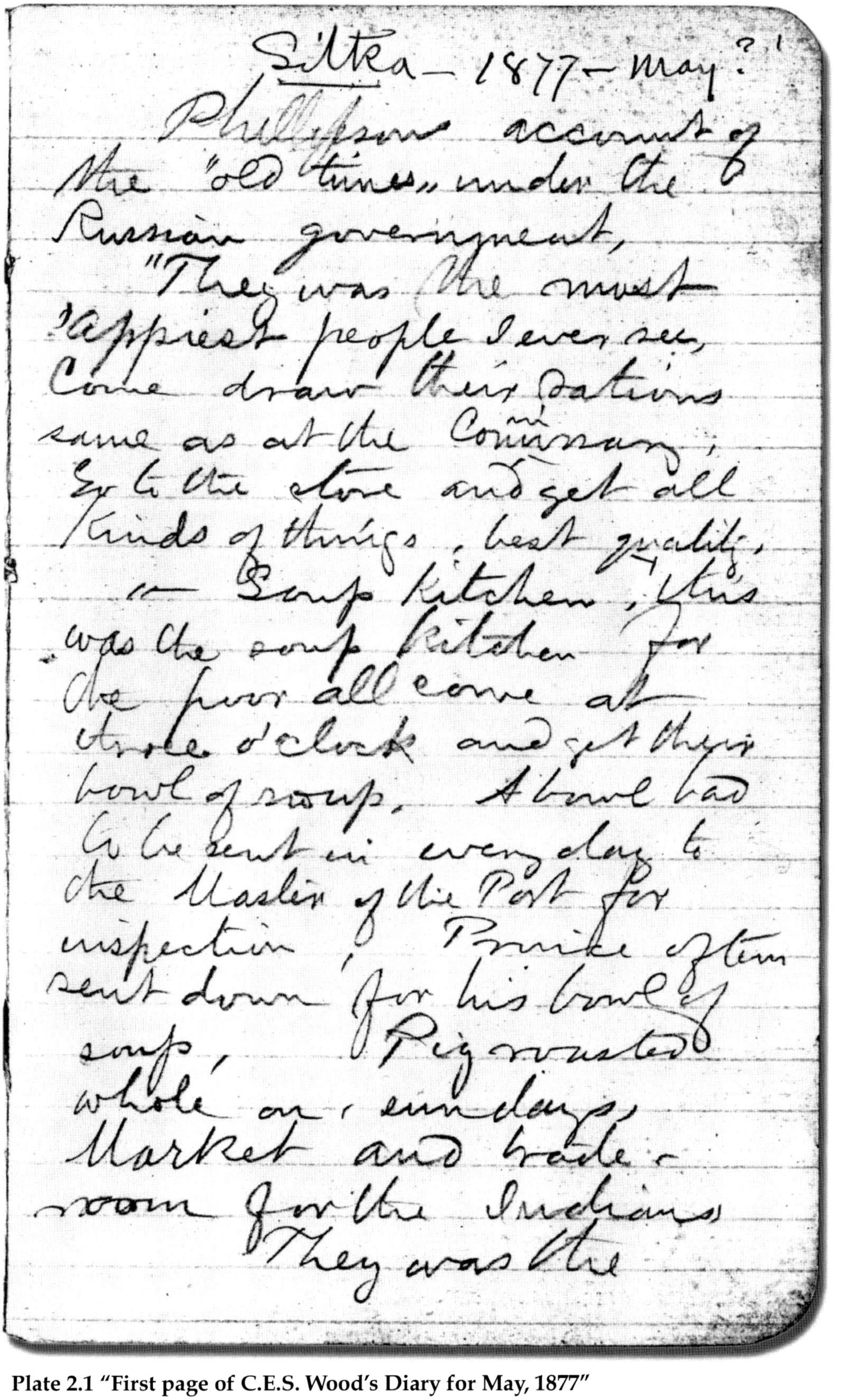

PART II. THE SOLDIER'S DIARY: FACING THE PROBABILITIES BY WRITING

> Sitka — 1877 — May ?
>
> Phillipson's account of the "old times" under the Russian government,
>
> "They was the most 'appiest people I ever see, Come draw their rations same as at the Commisary, Go to the store and get all kinds of things, best quality,
>
> Soup Kitchen, this was the soup kitchen for the poor all come at twelve o'clock and get their bowl of soup. A bowl had to be sent in every day to the Master of the Port for inspection, Prince often sent down for his bowl of soup. Pig roasted whole on Sundays, Market and trade room for the Indians, They was the

Plate 2.1 "First page of C.E.S. Wood's Diary for May, 1877"

— cultural differences, ethnicity, terrain, self-destruction, mortality. All these encounters made that summer and fall of 1877 unforgettable.

Converting these thirty diary pages into publishable post-war texts would present numerous problems. For one, Erskine wrote rapidly and briefly in pencil, mixing military and private diction in an idiosyncratic shorthand — fragments, abbreviations, dashes, symbols, numbers, quotations, allusions, lower case letters, no months, few place names. Reading his own writing here might have been difficult and the original text shows that — sometime later — he added dates and details.

To decode that difficult shorthand and revision, I've done the following: standardized spelling, mechanics, and date script; added [in brackets] month and place names, Army campsites, and captions; added paragraphs to longer passages; noted indecipherable words with [illegible], and arbitrary choices with [lost? last?]. When Erskine underlined, I use [Wood's emphasis]. All of Erskine's post-war revisions in ink — dates, overstrikes, additions, marginalia, interlineations — are enclosed in {+*italics*}, as is his one major 1878 revision. All of Erskine's deletions are enclosed in {–*italics*}.[4]

After the war, as Lt. Wood, he also had to decide what he should choose and what he should avoid in publishing pieces based on these entries. As Lt. Wood, he could not publicly criticize Gen. Howard — who had trusted him sufficiently to promote him to aide-de-camp on July 22. He also had to decide how to portray the non-treaty Nez Perce — people he came to respect and admire during this summer. Finally, as Erskine, he had to decide whether or not to expand on, further reveal, or suppress his personal responses, his inner life, his own observations. As Part III shows, he wrestled with these questions for the rest of his life.

---

4. Published here by permission, the original diary is housed in the Wood Collection, WD Box 26(1), Huntington Library, San Marino, California, where it was deposited by Sara Bard Field with Wood's other papers sometime after 1947. "C. E. S. Wood Diary, 1877: Alaska and Nez Perce War."

{+*Sitka 1877- May ?*}

Phillipson's account of the "old times" under the Russian government: "They was the most happiest people I ever see. Come draw their rations same as at the Commissary, go to the store and get all kinds of things. Best quality.[5]

"Soup kitchen: this was the soup kitchen for the poor. All come at three o'clock and get their bowl of soup. A bowl had to be sent in every day to the Master of the Port for inspection. Prince often sent down for his bowl of soup.[6] Pig roasted whole on Sundays. Market and trade room for the Indians.

"They was the most virtuous people I ever see in a seaport."

Contrast now: the poor old loafing clerk with nothing to do; the old musician. Day off. Drunkenness, squalor, debauchery, prostitution, stagnation, filth and all uncleanness. Unreliability of the men for work. Prostitution a necessity.

Berry's discussion on drunkenness: "I've got no use for drunkard around me. Been a millionaire if I hadn't had twice on four drunkards for partners. Good fellows too. Couldn't shake 'em.[7]

"There's old Smith. Baldy Smith we used to call him because he was bald. Made some $15,000, left ranching came to town, started saloon keeping, married a woman fit for no man's wife. She wasn't a bad [Wood's emphasis] woman. Had a baby every three or four hours. And a filthy dirty slovenly slut. Perfect bitch about the house. Smith drank himself to death, left his wife and six children, three of 'em his, went down to Astoria the other day and drowned himself."[8]

"There's Dr. Wilcox. Perfect gentleman, good friend of mine, fine gentleman he was too. Committed suicide in Portland the other day. He'd carry that thing full of whisky inside of him and you'd meet him on the street and think him perfectly sober, but he couldn't stand it you know. Killed him. Damn the stuff. No man of happiness can afford to drink whisky. An occasional tear is bad enough for any man but an habitual drinker will never die rich."[9]

Lewis having his horse stolen, offered $2.50 for his saddle, and drops it in the Deschutes in disgust.

Walker: "Injuns likes [sic] to catch the 'erring.' [herring]."

---

5. William Phillipson, a Sitka trader and schooner captain. He told Wood that "his schooner will return about the 15th of June and that he [Phillipson] is going to trade with the Chilcat chief at his village and that he will take me [Wood] along." C. E. S. Wood, letter to Gen. Howard, May 16, 1877. Oliver Otis Howard Papers, Bowdoin College Library, Brunswick, Maine. Appointed Postmaster in Sitka, August 14, 1871, Phillipson died July 18, 1924. Karen Meizner, E-mail to author, March 4, 2004. Wood elided this surname to "Phillips" in his 1882 article.

5. William Phillipson, a Sitka trader and schooner captain. He told Wood that "his schooner will return about the 15th of June and that he [Phillipson] is going to trade with the Chilcat chief at his village and that he will take me [Wood] along." C. E. S. Wood, letter to Gen. Howard, May 16, 1877. Oliver Otis Howard Papers, Bowdoin College Library, Brunswick, Maine. Appointed Postmaster in Sitka, August 14, 1871, Phillipson died July 18, 1924. Karen Meizner, E-mail to author, March 4, 2004. Wood elided this surname to "Phillips" in his 1882 article.

6. Prince Dmitry Maksutov was Chief Manager for the Russian government from December, 1863, to October, 1867. C. L. Andrews, *Sitka: The Chief Factory of the Russian American Company*, 3rd ed. (Caldwell: Caxton, 1945), 88.

7. Probably Maj. M. P. Berry, a veteran of the Civil and Mexican wars, served as U. S. Collector of Customs in Sitka in 1877. Berry later requested that a Navy vessel be sent to Sitka. He was admitted to the Alaska bar in 1884. Andrews, Sitka, 112, n.10; Hubert Howe Bancroft, *History of Alaska* (San Francisco: History Company, 1886), 619.

8. Possible reference to Capt. Harry M. Smith, Company G, Twenty-first Infantry, who "Died at Fort Lapwai, Idaho Territory April 23, 1877 of inflammation of the stomach and bowels." Trevor K. Plante, National Archives and Records Administration, letter to author, April 14, 2004. In his next letter to Gen. Howard, Wood writes: "[Maj. Canby] says too that Smith of the 21st killed himself." Wood to Howard, May 16, 1877, Howard Papers. These frank diary notes show Erskine's uncensored writing for himself about taboo subjects and the letter shows his self-censorship as Lt. Wood when writing to Howard.

9. Dr. Ralph Wilcox was a "native of Ontario County, New York, who came to Oregon in 1845. He shot himself April 18, 1877, at age 58. Biography Card File, Oregon Historical Society Research Library, Portland [hereafter OHS Research Library].

June 11 [Sitka]

Monday Steamer [*California*] arrives.[10]

June {+*12–13*} [Sitka]

Rush of preparation to evacuate. Sale of goods and government stores. Mule sale.[11] Conversation at the priest's house. Fright of the wretched women. Madame Metropolsky's offer of subsistence for the troops. Her fears of attack and murder.[12]

June 14 [Sitka to Wrangel]

The leave taking. Mistresses and sweethearts. Soldier's parting with his child. The old Russian woman praying to be taken to portland {+*P*}. The tearful group on the wharf. Bring {+*ing*} in the drunks. Farewell to Sitka.

June 15

Wrangel. Scenes in Wrangel. Slavery in U.S. Slave difficulty on the ship. Sacrificing slaves & etc. Small Siwash smoking his meerschaum, old blind Paul. His opinion of the manufacturing of whisky: "Bad–fooling mighty bad, damn bad...."

Plate 2.2 "Sitka Harbor, U.S. Navy or Coast Guard Longboats, 1878."
Sailing north on the large ocean-going steamer *California*, Charles Taylor and Wood enter this harbor in mid-April, 1877. Writing four years later, Wood describes the vista: "The snowy cone of Edgecumbe first appeared, then the sharp peak of Vostovia — a triangular patch against the sky. Everywhere below the snow-line the mountains were green...The harbor was protected against the sea by a curved line of reefs, on which grew firs and pines and cedars...The warm moist atmosphere curtained the middle distance with a film of blue, and, in the foreground, a fleet of very graceful canoes, filled with naked or half-naked Indians, completed the illusion." ("Among the Thlinkits in Alaska" *Century* XXIV, 1882: 323).

---

10. The private ocean steamer that made monthly trips between Portland and Alaska.

11. After ten years of responsibility for Alaskan affairs — except customs, commerce, and navigation — the Army was withdrawing completely from this remote and expensive post. Wood probably knew men in Company M, Twenty-first Infantry, who were selling everything and boarding the southbound steamer. Paul T. Scheips, "Darkness and Light The Interwar Years 1865-1898," in *American Military History* (Washington, D.C.: U.S. Army Center of Military History, 1989), 296-97; R.N. DeArmond, E-mail to author, February 27, 2004.

12. "The priest's house" refers to the residence of the Russian Orthodox priest Father Nicholas G. Metropolsky who "presided over the church [Cathedral of St. Michael] for many years" and later helped to organize a local government and Sitka city charter. Like many Sitka residents, Madame Metropolsky feared that the U.S. military withdrawal would leave Sitka residents vulnerable to a Tlingit attack similar to an earlier attack that had driven out the Russians. There was no Tlingit attack. Andrews, *Sitka*, 70; Dr. Charles Coate, E-mail to author, February 21, 2004; Meizner, E-mail to author, March 4, 2005.

June 16 [Inside Passage]

Fair weather in morning, foggy rainy at night. Pass Metlakatla — Church and settlement — run through Grenville Channel.[13] {*–Did you see her looking for gloves under the cattle when she first came in? Hadn't lost her gloves at all.*}

June 17 {*–& 18*} [Inside Passage to Port Townsend]

Still progressing southward. Pass through Seymour Narrows morning of 18 {*–17*} about 3:30 o'clock. Hard wind. Party around smoke stack in cruel glee over the sufferings of the seasick doctors. Baker's exasperation: "Why don't the old scoundrel take her out of the trough of the sea?" Arrive at Fort Townsend in evening. Visit Dr. Alden and Scrubby and go to bed.[14]

Plate 2.3: "Sitka Dock, 1878." Four years after docking here, Wood described the scene: "When we landed at Sitka, we forced our way through a crowd of Indians, Russians, half-breeds, Jews, and soldiers, to whom this monthly arrival is life itself, and went directly to the trading-store and post office." (Wood, Thlinkits, 324.) On this dock in 1877, Wood watches the U.S. Army withdraw and observes the frightened civilians.

---

13. "Church and settlement" refer to Father Duncan's Tsimshian mission. Duncan believed Native peoples needed to be isolated from white civilization and degeneracy until they could be prepared for assimilation. He pushed prohibition, adoption of the English language, and abandonment of Native culture. He later moved his settlement to New Metlakatla near Ketchikan. Coate, E-mail to author, February 21, 2004.

14. Baker was Acting Assistant Surgeon William D. Baker. See William G. Morris, *Report Upon the Customs District, Public Service, and Resources of Alaska Territory* (Washington, D.C.: Government Printing Office, 1879), 25. Dr. Charles Alden was a U.S. Army surgeon assigned to Fort Townsend. The 1877 Territorial Census listed "Mrs. Alden 37, and four children, 10-2." Scrubby may be the nickname of Lt. Ebenezer W. Stone, Twenty-first Infantry, who served as post commander. Plante, letter to author, April 7, 2004; Victoria Davis, E-mail to author, March 23, 2004.

June 19 {–20} [Port Townsend to Columbia River]
 Put Bancroft and his Company ashore at Townsend and take Burton and his Company aboard. Rumors of war. Touch at Townsend, sound Flattery light and put to sea.[15]

June 20 {–21} [Astoria to Portland]
 Cross the bar, touch at Canby's.[16] The telegram. Stirring news. No companies to disembark. All under orders for the front. Discharge the baggage and sick. Farewell to [Fort] Canby. Touch at Astoria and {–all we} hear reports of Perry's massacre with his command.[17] Growing excitement. Cheering remarks from citizens of, "Go in and kill'em all boys. Don't spare the bloody savages." Confound these curses. Wish they were going to fight them instead of standing on a wharf and put us on the track.[18]

 Arrive in Portland at about 2 o'clock at night. Round up {+Col. Adjut} Wood and get news and orders.[19] I visit Mrs. Howard.[20] General well. Perry not killed. Theller of mine {+21st} killed.[21] Volunteers called for. All troops ordered up.

---

15. Capt. Eugene A. Bancroft, Company M, Fourth Artillery, was stationed at Fort Townsend; Capt. George H. Burton, Company C, Twenty-first Infantry, at Fort Vancouver.

16. Fort Canby, Washington, at the mouth of the Columbia River. See Lewis A. MacArthur and Lewis L. MacArthur, *Oregon Geographic Names*, 7th ed. (Portland: OHS Press, 2003), 155. As judge advocate, Wood had been here before.

17. Capt. David L. Perry stationed at Fort Lapwai. On June 17, Perry led one hundred three men of the First Cavalry into battle against a force of 60-70 Nez Perce warriors. Ignorant of terrain and unskilled in war, Perry's men were routed by veteran Nez Perces, who were superior horsemen, marksmen, and tacticians. Perry's command panicked and retreated, leaving behind thirty-four dead soldiers — though Perry himself survived the so-called "Battle of White Bird Canyon." Greene, *Nez Perce Summer,1877* (Helena: Montana Historical Society Press, 2000), 25-48.

18. This is the first explicit evidence of Wood's ambivalence toward aggression.

19. Col. Henry Clay Wood, Assistant Adjutant General, stationed at Fort Vancouver. In 1875-76, he had researched and written the definitive report arguing that "because Joseph's band had never signed the 1863 agreement [treaty]...the band could not be forced to move.... Howard was so impressed...that he wrote to the War Department, 'I think it a great mistake to take from Joseph and his band of Nez Perces Indians that valley [the Wallowa].'" Bruce Hampton, *Children of Grace* (New York: Henry Holt, 1994), 42; U.S. Army, Dept. of the Columbia, *The Status of Young Joseph and His Band of Nez Perce Indians*...(Portland, Oregon: Assistant Adjutant General's Office, Department of Columbia, 1876).

20. Elizabeth Anne Waite married Oliver Otis Howard in 1855, a year after he graduated from West Point. She welcomed and treated Wood as a family member — evidenced here by his visit.

21. 1st Lt. Edward R. Theller, Twenty-first Infantry, stationed at Fort Lapwai. Killed on June 17 at White Bird, he had been Perry's subordinate officer.

June {+21} [Portland to Celilo]

Off for the front. Bancroft's Company on board with us — once more.[22] Meet the [steamer] *Canby* and pick up Throckmorton and Rodney with his Company.[23] Now we have five Companies in all. Touch at Vancouver. Say howdy do and goodbye in a breath. Take on some of the munitions of war — field pieces and gatlings and howitzers.

Cascades at noon. Party of admiring damsels gaze on the defenders of the country. Wainwright in desperation.[24] Paddock's advice to him: "Come along and telegraph for permission, and if permission is refused at that end, begin to telegraph to the General at Lewiston."[25] Anything to gain time and keep moving to the front.

Arrive at Dalles in evening. Feel {–*Felt feel*} very much like staying in Dalles and keeping some of the pretty girls that look so favorably upon us from any sadness or anxiety on *my* [Wood's emphasis] account.[26] Buy a hat in Dalles. First opportunity to purchase anything whatever since I left Sitka. Everything I own, blankets and clothes are all in my boxes in hold of *California*.

Through to Celilo. The poor Indians on the rocks of The Dalles wave encouraging signals to us to go on and kill and be killed. Hard to tell which they prefer. Leave Celilo about seven o'clock in the evening and at last are on a boat where we remain for two days and two nights and can take a rest. One week from Sitka to Celilo. Whoopla!

---

22. "When the *California* left the posts in Alaska on the 16th of June, she had on board 'A,' 'G,' and 'M' companies of the Fourth Artillery. Three days laters [*sic*], she stopped at Fort Townsend, near the mouth of Puget Sound, to discharge 'M' Company and take on 'C' Company of the 21st Infantry. The boat was hardly out of sight before Captain Eugene A. Bancroft, commanding 'M' company, received his orders. Taking a boat to Tacoma, and a train thence to Kaloma [*sic*] on the Columbia River, 'M' Company rejoined their comrades at Portland." Mark H. Brown, *The Flight of the Nez Perce* (New York: Putnam, 1967), 145.

23. Capt. Charles B. Throckmorton, Fourth Artillery, and Capt. George B. Rodney, Company D, Fourth Artillery. See "Accounts Page A" for Wood's tally of these men.

24. 2nd Lt. Robert P. Page Wainwright, Company K, First Cavalry, stationed at The Dalles. In September, 1877, Wainwright participated in the re-burial of soldiers killed at White Bird. In 1879, he was stationed at Fort Walla Walla. *Roster of Troops Serving in the Department of the Columbia* (Vancouver: U.S. Army, August, 1879), 5; Greene, *Nez Perce Summer*, 390n48.

25. 1st Lt. George H. Paddock, Fourth Artillery, later involved in a "friendly fire" death. See July 6 entry and note.

26. These and later paragraphs further reveal Wood's ambivalence about aggression.

Plate 2.4 "The *Almota* on the Columbia." Boarding this new upriver steamer *Almota*, Wood and the boatload of fellow soldiers rest and eat and sleep comfortably as they sail the Columbia above Celilo, then up the Snake River to Lewiston. Soldiers and passengers in this photo are unidentified. Date unknown.

{+*June 1877*} in left margin

{+*June '77*} in top margin

June 22 [Celilo to Snake River]

En route aboard the [steamer] *Almota*. Touch at Umatilla. News — sixty men missing. Troops camped near Lewiston. Lapwai said to be abandoned. Heard that at Dalles yesterday. Don't believe it.

June 23 {+3} [Snake River to Lewiston]

Nearing the field. Peculiar nervous feeling of going to death. Shrinking from the exposure. [Want? Most?] desire to be out of the expedition. Old soldiers the same way. Each fight more dreaded than the last. The desire to investigate immortality. Thoughts of death, inability to change the mood and tenor of life and thoughts. Each one's expectation that *he* [Wood's emphasis] will escape.[27]

---

27. Greene notes that this entry provides "rare contemporary insight into the emotions of soldiers bound for the front during an Indian campaign..." (*Nez Perce Summer*, 389). Greene deciphers Wood's handwriting somewhat differently than given here. Smith transcribes as "Most...." *The View From Officers' Row*, 139.

Plate 2.5 "Fort Lapwai, Idaho Territory." Attributed to "an Officer of Gen. Howard's Staff," *The Daily Graphic* in New York fills the front page on August 3, 1877, with this sketch, Gen. Howard's portrait, and nine other drawings. Leaking these eleven images, Wood intends to publicize Howard's story after he is criticized for defeats by the Nez Perces.

June 24
Arrival at Lewiston. Bustle of preparation. Lapwai.[28]

---

28. Wood may have sketched Fort Lapwai while passing through. Here, he may also have received the standard forty pounds or so of infantry equipment that he lists in "Accounts Pages" at the end of this diary. As an officer, Wood was required to purchase a rifle, ammunition belt, and canteen. For a heroic depiction of uniformed infantry marching — as Wood probably marched — see Plate 2.6.

Plate 2.6 "In Pursuit of Joseph" by Vincent Colyer. In contrast with Wood's journal, Colyer here idealizes infantry power, order, and confidence in the vicinity of Fort Lapwai — probably before the White Bird defeat. A former Board of Indian Commissioners member, active artist, YMCA activist, and a zealous Christian assimilationist, Colyer was touring northwest Indian reservations that summer. (*Harper's Weekly*, August 18, 1877.)

June 25 [Fort Lapwai to Norton's Ranch/Cottonwood]

Arrival of pack trains. Incidents in packing, comic and serio comic. 25th. Troops start for the front. Mrs. F's description of her Indian scare — in the cellar.[29]

June 26 [Norton's Ranch to White Bird Creek]

A new pack train. On the road. Rodney's camp. The nest of officers in one tent. Pouring rain. Night ride in cold drenching rain. Hail. Camp at Norton's. Norton's pup. Deserted houses, flowers and chickens uncared for. Milk pails left on the fence. Evidence of a hurried flight.[30]

---

29. Mrs. F. is Emily FitzGerald, wife of Army surgeon Dr. Jenkins FitzGerald. She apparently told Wood how, four "days after the rout at White Bird[,] some white ruffians chased and fired on two friendly Indians who promptly whipped their ponies to top speed and dashed to the post [Fort Lapwai.] Before their excited remarks could be properly interpreted, the cry spread that the hostiles were coming; the troops took up defensive positions, and the wives of enlisted men and their children 'came running, wild with fear, to the officers' line of houses' where 'a block house had been established..., and casks of water and provisions were kept in the cellar. Cord wood had been stacked around the house to protect it from shot and all the women and children had been instructed in case of attack to take shelter there.'" Brown, *Flight of the Nez Perce*, 141. For greater insight about Emily FitzGerald, see Smith, *The View From Officers' Row*, 144.

30. The ranch was established on Nez Perces land in 1862 by some of the 20,000 invading gold miners. Originally called "Cottonwood House" and later "Norton's Ranch"after then-owner Benjamin B. Norton, the ranch straddled the Lewiston-Mount Idaho road and included barns, stables, and corrals, as well as a "store, saloon, hotel, and stage station." The Norton family and others had fled the ranch for Grangeville on the night of June 14. Alvin Josephy, *The Nez Perce Indians and the Opening of the Northwest* (New Haven: Yale University Press, 1965) 386-442; Greene, *Nez Perce Summer*, 32 and 59; Brown quotes from but does not credit this diary entry (*Flight of the Nez Perce*, 157).

{+*June 27*} [Whitebird Battlefield to Camp Theller on Salmon River][31]

Graves by the wayside. Overtaking the main column. Gentlemanly officers looking like herders. Rough aspect of everyone. Business — not holiday — costumes.[32]

Burying the dead {+*in White Bird Canyon*}.[33] Horrible stench. Arms and cheeks gone. Bellies swollen. Blackened faces. Mutilations.[34] Heads gone. Tragic fate of the bugler. Indian atrocities. Ravishing and burning women. The man of 14 days — gooseberry his [illegible].

Camp. Singing, storytelling and swearing. Profanity — carelessness — accepting things — horrible at other times. As a matter of course, each as mutilated corpses and death in ghastly forms, strewn on every side. Again there is the necessary leaving of last messages for sweethearts, mothers, and wives, telling of {–*mementoes*} jokes about being killed, about not looking for "my body" and etc. Firing expected tomorrow. The nerve it takes to face the probabilities by writing these last letters and leaving mementoes for loved ones is wonderful — and one feels demoralized by such acts as these.

Rain — eternal rain — veal and no veal. Supper in camp. Visiting at the different messes. Youngsters with neither bedding nor shelter. Roughing it jokingly. Night duty. Posting the pickets. Rough times all night standing in the rain. No fire. No talking. No bedding. No sleeping. Up at two o'clock for fear of Indian habits of attack. Roll call at six. (The alarm shot at midnight. One of our own pickets shot by one of our men.)[35] Breakfast.

---

31. Brown quotes this entire day's entry as providing "an intimate picture of this camp" and credits Wood anonymously (*Flight of the Nez Perce*, 159-61). See also Robert Hamburger, *Two Rooms*, 46; Greene, *Nez Perce Summer*, 45-46; and Hampton, *Children of Grace*, 90: all quote excerpts and give in-text credit. Greene deciphers Wood's handwriting somewhat differently than given here.

32. Wood's Company D, Twenty-first Infantry, and the four other companies from the *Almota* joined Gen. Howard's other forces on this day — the second day of burials. Brown, *Flight of the Nez Perce*, 160-61; John D. McDermott, *Forlorn Hope* (Boise: Idaho State Historical Society, 1978), 123-24.

33. Wood's unpublished poem, "Ballad of the Burials," and passages in published *The Poet in the Desert* arise from this burial detail at White Bird Canyon. The soldiers' naked bodies had lain unburied for ten days.

34. Wood records Army misperception here. Citing Lucullus V. McWhorter, *Hear Me, My Chiefs: Nez Perce Legend and History* (Caldwell, Idaho: Caxtons, 1952), 256-259, Alvin Josephy states the prevailing view: "Despite stories that circulated to the contrary, none of the bodies...were discovered to have been mutilated." Josephy, *Nez Perce Indians*, 531.

35. Jerome Greene explains that "During the movement of Howard's forces to and below the Salmon River, two inadvertent army shootings occurred that, because of the limited information available about them, have caused considerable confusion. The first was the accidental wounding of Pvt. Henry Reed, Company E, First Cavalry...Reed was mistakenly shot in the shoulder by an infantry picket [unidentified] and was taken to the post hospital at Fort Lapwai, where he was recuperating as of July 30, 1877." Greene, "Appendix B, *Two Army Shootings at the Salmon River*, June 30 and July 7, 1877," unpublished manuscript, *Historic Resource Study: The U.S. Army and the Nee-Me-Poo Crisis of 1877: Historic Sites Associated with the Nez Perce War*. (Denver: National Park Service, 1996,) 702-10; Greene, *Nez Perce Summer*, 391n1. For the second shooting, see entry July 6, page 40.

{+*June 28*} [Camp Theller at Salmon River (East Bank)]

The advance. More ruins. Indians speckling the hills like ants. Firing.[36] Sudden feeling of interaction on hearing the shots. Nervous eagerness for the fight. Desire to be at the front. All thoughts of the future vanishing. Only want a crack at an Indian[37] and feel no disposition to show any quarter. Advance to river. Planted batteries and left picket lines commanding the crossing. Rodney encamps at Camp Theller.[38] Artillery remains in position. E and I Companies return with Cavalry to camp.

{+*June 29*} [Salmon River at White Bird Crossing]

Entire command moves to river. Attempt to cross the river.[39]

{+*June 30*} [Salmon River at White Bird Crossing]

Still constructing the ferry. Cavalry leave us for Looking Glass.[40] My farewell to Rains.[41] Wilkinson and Mason come up.[42] D, E, I, and part of Artillery cross this day.

---

36. The fleeing non-treaty bands — more than six hundred men, women, children, and around fifteen hundred horses — had crossed the Salmon on June 19. The gunfire Wood reports here came from rearguard scouts who "rode out from the canyons and from behind the buttes and came charging down the slope. They pulled up opposite the soldiers....Some of the soldiers began shooting, and the Indians fired back. None of the bullets found a mark, and a few moments later, when the Nez Perces saw Howard's artillerymen coming down the bluff with the howitzer, they broke off the fight" and rejoined the main non-treaty camp in the mountains. Josephy, *Nez Perce Indians*, 532.

37. Hamburger uses this phrase to title his chapter on Wood's Nez Perce conflict experience (*Two Rooms*, 41-58). After his recent Alaska experience with Native peoples, including sexual intimacy with "the niece of a powerful Chilkaht leader," it seems doubtful that Wood "hurried exuberantly" to the war, or that he felt "mounting anticipation at the prospect of seeing his first combat" as Hamburger claims (*Two Rooms*, 39). This phrase may be better understood as reactionary bravado rather than bellicose passion.

38. Gen. Howard's campsite a "mile or two above the mouth of White Bird Creek" and named for 1st Lt. Edward Theller whose body Wood and other soldiers had found and buried earlier that day. Brown, *Flight of the Nez Perce*, 160.

39. At spring flood stage, the river created a formidable obstacle to Howard's pursuit. Securing three boats, a 'practical ferryman' attempted to rig a rope ferry." Brown, *Flight of the Nez Perce*, 163.

40. Wood omits many complications: inadequate pulley, improvised shackles, breaking rope, spliced rope, exhausting rowing. This three-day delay was one reason the Nez Perces would name Gen. Howard "General Day After Tomorrow." See Plate 2.7. The reference to Looking Glass alludes to Capt. Whipple's completely unjustified attack July 1 on Chief Looking Glass' peaceful village along Clear Creek — well inside the 1863 reservation boundary. All sources agree that the "ill-conceived and poorly executed attack...netted the army nothing but another complication...[because] the chief — previously an advocate of peace — aligned his fortunes with those of White Bird, Joseph, and the others." Greene, *Nez Perce Summer*, 58.

41. Rains is 2nd Lt. Sevier M. Rains, probably Wood's contemporary at West Point: Wood graduated in 1874 and Rains in 1876. Four years after the war, Gen. Howard described Rains as "prompt, loyal, able, without fear, and without reproach." Oliver Otis Howard, *Nez Perce Joseph* (Boston: Lee and Shepard, 1881), 151.

42. 1st Lt. Melville C. Wilkinson, Third Infantry, an artillery man serving as an aide-de-camp to Gen. Howard; Maj. Edwin C. Mason, Twenty-first Infantry, stationed at Fort Vancouver, and Gen. Howard's Chief of Staff "supervising the placement of troops." Greene, *Nez Perce Summer*, 81. For Mason's letters from this conflict, see Stanley R. Davison, "A Century Ago: The Tortuous Pursuit," *Montana, The Magazine of Western History* 27, 4 (1977): 3-29.

Plate 2.7 "U.S. Troops Crossing Salmon River Rapids." Wood originally printed this caption in the lower left corner. Later, he wrote in longhand a second caption in the upper right sky. Wood spent June 29 through July 1 at White Bird Crossing and returned here to cross again on July 8 and 9. Possibly because the sketch depicts Army delay, he didn't send it to the eastern press. About 9x12 inches, the drawing is currently Wood's only signed original from 1877 and the only depiction of this activity. This drawing also confirms Wood carried or obtained pad, pencils, ink, pens.

July 1 [Salmon River at White Bird Crossing]

(Sunday). Remainder of troops cross this day.

July 2 [West Bank, Salmon River to Deer Creek Canyon]

Moved to point 3/4th way to summit of Snake river mountains.[43] Rain. Mud. Forty five degree ascent. {–Show} Bombarded with pack mules. Dead Mule Trail.[44] Return to pack trains. Camp Misery. Sleeping in water. [illegible].

July 3 [Deer Creek Canyon to Brown's Mountain(Camp Mountain)][45]

Mountain camp finally reached after long toil over Dead Mule Trail.

July 4 [Brown's Mountain to Camp Rains on Johns Creek][46]

March fifteen miles. We camp in sight of Mount Idaho. News of Rains disaster.[47] Duncan and Eltonhead fighting.[48] Camp. Rains.

Plate 2.8 "On Trail Near the Salmon River, July 2, 1877." In contrast with the *Harper's* cover, this cartoonish post-war sketch by Second Lieutenant Guy Howard understates the Army's ascent of Deer Creek Canyon, a march that Guy did not make. Arriving in Lewiston on July 22, Guy served with Wood as Gen. Howard's aide-de-camp to the end of the pursuit.

---

43. These mountains are now commonly demonized as the "Seven Devils" or "Seven Devil Range."

44. This place name — apparently Wood's unique non-military appellation — seems to have only been used (1) by Wood in this diary, and (2) in the drawing caption, "Dead Mule Trail, Idaho – From a Sketch by an Army Officer." (See Plate 2.9) Brown cites this entry and uses Wood's term, "Camp Misery" (*Flight of the Nez Perce*, 170).

45. Referred to as "Brown's Mountain," and as "Camp Howard Ridge." Cheryl Wilfong, *Following the Nez Perce Trail* (Corvallis: Oregon State University Press, 1990),100; McDermott, 112, n. c.); A Portland journalist adds, "The place of our camp was extremely cold, the entire command being overcoated and huddled around immense pine wood camp fires during our entire stay." Thomas Sutherland, *Portland Daily Standard*, July 16, 1877.

46. "On the Fourth of July...we reached a campground in a pine forest which General Howard named after Lieutenant Rains, who was killed while performing perilous scout duty in the neighborhood of Camas Prairie." Sutherland, *Daily Standard*, July16, 1877.

47. Rains and his scouting party of ten soldiers were killed on July 3 at Cottonwood. The "Nez Perces were about to launch a surprise attack against the main soldier body, when they... sight[ed] the smaller troop riding out from the command [, so] they pursued the scouting party...and eventually all were dispatched" by Strong Eagle, Yellow Wolf, Two Moons, Five Wounds, Rainbow, and other warriors. Merrill D. Beal, *I Will Fight No More Forever* (Seattle: University of Washington Press, 1963), 68; McWhorter, *Hear Me*, 282-286.

48. Lieutenants Joseph W. Duncan and Francis E. Eltonhead, both 21st Infantry, both stationed at Fort Walla Walla.

Plate 2.9 "Dead Mule Trail, Idaho." Attributed as "From a Sketch by an Army Officer," this September 29 *Harper's* cover is probably based on a Wood original depicting the wet, muddy 10-mile uphill climb out of Deer Creek and the deaths of four pack mules. Apparently, a magazine staff artist revised Wood's original to sensationalize the Army with wild west stereotypes.

Plate 2.10 "*Left to right*: **James Reuben, Mark Williams, and Archie B. Lawyer.**" Wood met Reuben and wrote down some of his stories when the treaty Nez Perce became a scout, adviser, and interpreter for Gen. Howard. Taken a year later, this 1878 photo depicts Reuben with two Christianized Nez Perces appointed as teachers for Chief Joseph's people exiled in Oklahoma. Standing behind them is Indian Agent for the Lapwai Reservation, John B. Montieth.

July 5 [Johns Creek to Salmon River at Craig Billy Crossing][49]

Move to Camp Otis on Salmon. Twelve miles below Camp Haughey. Raft.[50] Alarm by Lear[y?].[51] Arrival of "Ruben"{+ *friendly Nez Perce*}.[52] On Picket.[53] {–"*Crusoe Otis*"}

---

49. "This crossing, at the mouth of Billy Creek, had once been the home of the Nez Perce Indian known as Salmon River Billy. His son, Luke Billy, now lived there in a cabin. But a ferry had also existed at the site during the gold rush, and a good trail still led from the crossing toward Craig Mountain and the main road between Lewiston and Camas Prairie. Hence the name of the place, which was also called Craig's Ferry." Josephy, *Nez Perce Indians*, 535, n.10. Attempting to avoid violence, the fleeing non-treaty bands and their livestock had crossed here on July 2 — three days earlier.

50. Refers to the Army's dismantling of Luke Billy's cabin to build a raft for crossing the Salmon. "Its timbers were a foot thick and thirty or forty feet long. Twenty-three years after the war, Luke Billy was still trying to collect from the government for its loss." Bill Gulick, *Chief Joseph Country* (Caldwell: Caxtons, 1981), 212.

51. Possible reference to an unidentified action by 1st Lt. Peter Leary, Howard's "purchasing agent for commissary supplies." Brown, *Flight of the Nez Perce*, 303.

52. James Ruben, a bi-lingual Christianized treaty Nez Perce, was "the son of old Ruben, who had operated a ferry and grown wealthy during the gold rush, and of Joseph's sister." An interpreter and messenger prior to the conflict, he became a scout, adviser, and interpreter for Gen. Howard. On this day at Craig's Ferry, Ruben demonstrated how to cross the Salmon River with his horse — a feat Howard's troops could not accomplish. Josephy, *Nez Perce Indians*, 486; Howard, *Nez Perce Joseph*, 150.

53. A letter by Wood's commanding officer describes the situation: "The company along with Lt. Woods [sic], three Indian scouts and myself have been on picket duty last night on the side of the mountain overlooking the vicious Salmon River.... Our duty is to see that no Indians steal on us or surprise the camp or command in a scalping bee while in the act of preparing our crossing of the river." Robert Pollock, *Grandfather, Chief Joseph, and Psychodynamics* (Caldwell: Caxton, 1964), 57-58.

HOW THE TE-TAW-KEN CAME TO BE.

James Reuben, with the scarred mouth and deep voice — he who fought with us against Chief Joseph and was wounded at Lo-Lo-Pass, who after the surrender joined the prisoners and begged for them until he had leave to bring some of the women and children from the Indian Territory back to their homes, — told me this tale.

THE name of the Nez Perces is *Te-taw-ken* — We the people. Once upon a time there were four giants and their giant sister who lived in the Salmon River and Palouse country. The sister wanted some otter liver to make big medicine. The great otter lived in the Palouse, which was a smooth river at that time, from the Snake to its head. So the four brothers took their spears and bows and went to hunt him. They stationed themselves along the river; and the lowest, seeing the great beast asleep, shot an arrow into him. At this the otter fell into the water and shivered. This made the first rapids of the Palouse. As the otter swam up-stream, the next brother also shot an arrow into him; again he shivered, and this made the second rapids. Still he swam upstream, lashing the water into foam with his tail; and the third brother shot him. At this he made some tremendous struggles, and thus came the rapids just below the falls. At this time the last giant ran down and thrust his spear through the otter; and the dying animal tore up the earth and rocks, and threw them about like sand. This made the falls of the Palouse. Then the sister cut the beast into pieces, and threw some here, some there; where a piece fell there was made a band of the *Chu-te-pa-lus* or *Ne-me-pus* nation, Cayuses, Spokanes, Okanokanes, Umatillas, Walla Wallas. But the Nez Perces themselves, the *Te-taw-ken*, who are truly the people, they came from the strong heart of the otter. Then when the giants saw the earth was filled with brave men (*homonick*), they took stations to watch over them; and, standing so long on guard, they were turned into mountains. There they still stand, white snow mountains above the earth.

Plate 2.11 "How the Te-Taw-Ken Came To Be." Wood apparently wrote down Reuben's version of two Nez Perce myths, saved them with similar tales he collected during the 1870's from Alaska and Southeast Oregon. In 1901, Wood's son Maxwell and a friend published a limited edition of these narratives; in 1929, that collection was reprinted for a wider audience as *A Book of Indian Tales* (New York: Vanguard Press), with this text on pp. 81-83.

July 6 [Craig Billy Crossing to Salmon River Mountains (Camp Parnell)]

"Crusoe Otis."[54] Arrival of pack train from Haughey. Horrible retrograde march. Camp at head of canyon. Soldier shot [by] {+*Lieutenant Paddock. Solemnity of the silent corpse, the simple grave, the soldier's burial clothes. The lonely mound under the mournful pines, and all the pathos of death in loneliness. How all things earthly sink into nothingness before the dread silence of the dead one.*}[55] "False Alarm."[56]

July 7 [Camp Parnell at Salmon River Mountains]

Long weary dragging march to mountain camp.[57] Cavalry and Headquarters leave us for Grangeville. Stragglers. Hard march.

July 8 [Salmon River Mountains to Salmon River at White Bird Crossing

March to river by shorter route. Avoid Dead Mule Trail. Overtake Cavalry and Headquarters. Put Cavalry over river and ferry our Infantry Battalion over. Cavalry and Headquarters and Haughey push on.

July 9 [West Bank, Salmon River, to East Bank and White Bird Canyon]

Artillery crosses. Command camps at "Theller." Hunting berries. Camp struck and {+*we*} push for the front. Night's march and our wretched "bivowk" [sic] at head of White Bird Canyon. No food. No anything.

---

54. Wood records the nickname — alluding to Defoe's novel *Robinson Crusoe* — given to Lt. Harrison Otis after his log raft "and the lariat ropes of the cavalry — all went down the river three or four miles. When the impromptu sailors returned, the shavetail [newly-commissioned West Point officer] was dubbed, quite appropriately, "Crusoe Otis." Brown, *Flight of the Nez Perce*, 185.

55. According to a published post-war "Court of Inquiry," Wood refers here to the second "friendly fire" incident — a fatal shooting that occurred the night of July 7. The soldier killed was Pvt. Michael Cassidy, Battery D, 4th Artillery. That night, Cassidy had been posted as a camp guard and "wrapped himself in a blanket," which looked like "the ordinary costume of the hostile Indians." Cassidy "went outside the camp limits, and ...while returning to the camp he attracted Lieutenant [George H] Paddock's notice, excited his suspicions by the stealthy and unusual manner of his approach, and that Lieutenant Paddock fired upon him under the impression that he was an Indian, with the result of killing Private Cassidy." Paddock was found to have "acted in good faith and that his action was warranted under the circumstances." *General Orders No. 8.*, Headquarters Department of the Columbia, Portland, Oregon, 9 February 1878. Wood moved his additional reflection on Cassidy's death from this 1877 Nez Perces War diary to an 1878 "literary notebook" — which he completed after the 1878 Paiute Bannock conflict. To show some of his revising, I have added — in italics — part of his July 9, 1878, entry to this 1877 entry. For the complete and previously-unidentified revision, see "C.E.S. Wood Private Journal, 1878." *Oregon Historical Quarterly* (March, 1969): 26-27. See also Greene, *Two Army Shootings*, pp. 702–710.

56. "[We] have just had an Indian scare. A man cam [sic] doubling down the trail crying The Indians are coming! The Indians are coming! I [illegible] this into [illegible] and commenced giving orders — in a few moments it was discovered to be a false alarm and with a hearty laugh everybody settled down again — " Maj. Edwin Mason to his wife, July 5,1877, pp. 3-4, Mason Correspondence, Microfilm 80, Montana Historical Society, Helena, Montana.

57. The march back to White Bird Crossing from Billy Craig Crossing is perhaps one of the most avoided three days in army narratives. Gen. Howard abstracted all three days into one (*Nez Perce Joseph*, 155). Thomas Sutherland, Portland journalist and one of Gen. Howard's post-war apologists, did much the same. Sutherland also rebutted Howard's critics by rationalizing the Army's inability to cross the Salmon as a tactical move: "They [the Nez Perces] had to be driven out [of the mountains] and they were." Thomas Sutherland, *Howard's Campaign against the Nez Perce Indians, 1877* (Portland: A.G. Walling, 1878), 4.

Plate 2.12 "The Howitzer in a Hot Place." Wood probably depicts the warriors' attack on the Fourth Artillery battery and two of the four casualties. In New York, the front page headline read, "General Howard's Battle With the Nez Perces Indians, July 11." Leaked to the eastern press without Army clearance, Wood's front page montage was attributed to "an Officer of General Howard's Staff." (*The Daily Graphic*, August 3, 1877, page 1.)

July 10 [White Bird Canyon to Walls at South Clearwater (East Bank)]

Take wagons for Grangeville. Arrive and breakfast. Our hostess Madame Crooks.[58] She cun [sic] talk. Proceed to General Howard's camp about six miles in rear of Indians. Crossing the Clearwater on the bridge. Wild flowers, tulips & etc. Duncan's [horse? house?].

July 11 [Walls to South Clearwater Battlefield (East Bank)]

Advance on Indians. Engage them at about 11:30 am. We occupying a rolling broken plateau. They the rocks and wooded ravines. Howitzers open fire. Skirmishing. Sharpshooting. Famous hat. The Sergeant and McNally shot. Charge by line in front of me. Firing till after dark. Indians in the ravines after horses. Caring for the wounded. No food no drink no clothing. All day without water. Night in the trenches. Preparing for an attack at dawn. Anxious times. Sound of Indians dancing and wailing. Williams and Bancroft shot.[59] I, [lost? last?] on the picket line. Incidents.

---

58. Passing through Grangeville again, Wood has now marched an oval of around ninety miles. Martha Crooks was the 55-year- old wife of "J. W. Crooks, cattle king and Grangeville promoter," and mother of eight children. McDermott, *Forlorn Hope*, 38-75; 1870 Census, Nez Perce County, Idaho.

59. Wood accurately describes the terrain where the semicircular battle line formed that afternoon. About one hundred non-treaty warriors and three hundred fifty army troops — cavalry, infantry, and artillery — fought through the hot afternoon without either side gaining a decisive advantage. Pvt. David McNally, Company E, Twenty-First Infantry, was one of eight soldiers killed; 2nd Lt. Charles A. Williams, Company C, Twenty-First Infantry, and Capt. Eugene A. Bancroft, Company A, Fourth Artillery, were two of twenty soldiers wounded. No exact number of Nez Perce casualties for this day is known. Greene, *Nez Perce Summer*, 77-88, 361-362.

Plate 2.13 "A Bold Charge on the Right." Another of his four sketches of the Battle of the Clearwater, Wood may depict here the first July 11 charge by mounted Nez Perce warriors led by Toohoolhoolzote. (*The Daily Graphic*, August 3, 1877, page 1.)

July 12 [East Bank, South Clearwater Battlefield][60]

Morning firing reopened. Jackson appearing.[61] Artillery withdrawn. Extending our line. The charge. Rapid firing. Indian works. Their camp captured. Preparing to follow. Our camp with the wounded. The Command camp [sic] on the river.[62]

---

60. During the second day of the battle, the non-treaty warriors attacked and retreated intermittently until artillerymen under Capt. Marcus J. Miller charged "double time across the plateau straight toward the warriors in the ravine." Cavalry and infantry — including Wood — followed Miller's charge, and the warriors retreated on horseback to the South Fork of the Clearwater, swam the river, and "raced their ponies up Cottonwood Creek and into the hills after their families." Known Nez Perces casualties for both July 11 and 12 were four warriors killed and six wounded. Greene, *Nez Perce Summer*, 88-96.

61. Capt. James Jackson, Company B, First Cavalry, who was escorting a "pack train of 120 mules and twenty Nez Perce scouts and Captain Birney B. Keeler, General McDowell's aide-de-camp...." from Fort Lapwai. Brown, *Flight of the Nez Perce*, 193.

62. Wood sketched four different events of this battle (see Plates 2.12–2.15). On August 3, 1877, these four sketches, Gen. Howard's studio portrait, and six other drawings — made up the entire front page of *The Daily Graphic* in New York. For his published account of this two-day battle, see "Chief Joseph, The Nez Perce," *Century Magazine* XXVIII, 1884: 135-42.

Plate 2.14 "Going to the Spring." During July 11, Nez Perce sharpshooters prevented the Army from getting to a cold spring — the sole source of water for men, horses, and mules. Here, Wood depicts the morning of July 12, when Capt. Miller, Capt. Perry, and Lt. Otis' gun battery are reclaiming the spring. (*The Daily Graphic,* August 3, 1877.)

Plate 2.15 "Attack on the Pack Train." The afternoon of July 11, Wood must have seen the warriors attack two civilian mule skinners and their pack train, which was about to deliver a load of howitzer ammunition. When the Nez Perces attacked, they killed two packers, and captured three mules and their baggage. Eventually, firing by cavalry drove off the warriors. This is another of Wood's nine front-page sketches published by *The Daily Graphic* on August 3, 1877.

Plate 2.16 "The Bivouac." Wood's sketch of a typical overnight camp somewhere in central Idaho. While this site is nameless, Army records show that Gen. Howard frequently named campsites to honor the service or memory of individuals. The signature "PhG Cusachs" in the lower left identifies the engraver who converted all ten of Wood's original paper sketches and Gen. Howard's studio photo for linotype press. (*The Daily Graphic*, August 3, 1877.)

July 13 [West Bank, South Clearwater, to Kamiah]

The pursuit. Hampered with howitzer ammunition. Crossing the river. The Indian camp.[63] Left behind with the howitzer ammunition. Losing the trail. Hearing the firing. View from the hills. Our doubts as to our position. Coming into camp. Indians across [*east of*] the river.[64]

July 14 [Kamiah (Camp McBeth)][65]

Still in camp. Indians across the river.

July 15 [Sunday, Kamiah]

Day off. Resting. Joseph wants to talk.[66] Wait all day. No talk. Begin to cross river in afternoon.

---

63. Writing to an Idaho historian forty some years after the war, Wood described the plundering of the Nez Perces' camp: "There were valuable buffalo-robes and beaded garments lying about in the teepees and meat cooking at the fire. I, myself, picked up a buffalo-horn drinking-cup hanging on a stick at the door of a teepee as we ran through the camp." Wood to C. J. Brosnan, January 7, 1918, Special Collections, University of Idaho Library, Moscow. After the war, he had that buffalo horn mounted in silver at Tiffany's with this inscription: "Taken from Chief Joseph's camp at the Battle of the Clear Water, July 13, 1877, by Lieut. C. E. S. Wood." Mary Rose, *C. E. S. Wood and Chief Joseph*...(Vancouver, Wash.: Celebrate Freedom Project, 1991-92), 14; see also Erskine Wood, *Life of Charles Erskine Scott Wood* (Vancouver, Wash.: Rose Wind Press, 1978), 14. This cup is preserved in the Erskine Wood Library, Law School, Lewis and Clark College, Portland.

64. Wood's unpublished poem, "Ballad of the Flight Across the Salmon River," memorializes Nez Perces skills at river crossing. "Ballads of the Nez Perce War." C. E. S. Wood Collection, WD Box 8 (16), Huntington Library.

65. Deciding to escape over Lolo Pass to Montana, the fleeing non-treaty bands were passing through the Indian agency and settlement when the soldiers attacked them again. After exchanging long-distance and mostly ineffectual gunfire across the river, both forces withdrew. Camp McBeth was named by Gen. Howard for Presbyterian missionary Kate McBeth, who fled to Lapwai at the outbreak of hostilities. [Author unknown], *Journal of Expedition against Hostile Nez Perce Indians, from Lewiston, I.T. to Henry's Lake, I.T., July 13, 1877*, WD Box 26 (2), Wood Collection [hereafter *Adjutant Journal*].

66. Kulkulsuitim, a messenger from Joseph, was talking with Gen. Howard and Maj. Mason about terms of surrender near the river when shots were fired at the officers. The parley ended. Joseph never appeared. Later, Howard imagined that this meeting was actually "a ruse designed to further impede the army while allowing the tribesmen time to move their noncombatants and livestock toward Lolo trail." Greene, *Nez Perce Summer*, 99-100.

Plate 2.17 "Indian Chief." One of the ten C. E. S. Wood sketches published August 3 in the New York press, this traditional Nez Perce leader remains unidentified by tribal officials and historians. He may be Red Heart, chief of the wrongfully imprisoned non-combatants. If so, Wood may have interviewed him and sketched him while serving as officer of the day on July 17. (*Daily Graphic*, August 3, 1877.)

July 16 [Kamiah to East Bank, Clearwater River]

Finish crossing the river. Go into a hot camp after being recalled from a march about a mile and a half. Prisoners begin to come in.[67] "Joseph halo come in," {+*no come in*}. Clatawa Lolo Trail."{+*gone away by Lolo Trail*}.[68] Cavalry start in pursuit. Rest for the weary sole.[69]

---

67. Wood echoes official diction here in using "prisoners" to name actual Nez Perce non-combatants caught in "one of the most unjust episodes of the Nez Perce War." Lucullus McWhorter, *Yellow Wolf* (Caldwell: Caxton Printers, 1940), 310. "Renown for their law-abiding and peaceful proclivities," Red Heart's band of thirty-five non-combatants — just returning from buffalo hunting in Montana — were designated "hostile" when they voluntarily surrendered, so Gen. Howard had this group arrested as "prisoners of war." Among these non-combatants were Chief Red Heart and Red Heart, Jr., who were present when Capt. Whipple and Companies E and L, First Cavalry, and twenty volunteers attacked — without provocation — Looking Glass's camp on Sunday morning, July 1. Josephy, *Nez Perce Indians*, 554-555; McWhorter, *Yellow Wolf*, 310-312; Brown, *Flight of the Nez Perce*, 204-05; McWhorter, *Hear Me, My Chiefs*, 331-334; Greene, *Nez Perce Summer*, 100, 408-409.

68. Wood quotes his translator's Chinook jargon which Wood — sometime later — added in English to the text.

69. This pun exemplifies Wood's sense of humor, a rare trait in 1877 Army diaries.

Plate 2.18 "Joseph Red Heart, 1906." Imprisoned with thirty-two other Nez Perce non-combatants at Ft. Vancouver from August, 1877, to April, 1878, Chief Red Heart was "respected by all the tribesmen as a man of dignity and honor." (McWhorter, *Hear Me, My Chiefs*, 333.)

July 17 [East Bank, Clearwater River at Kamiah]

Military commission formed to try prisoners.[70] Still they come. {–18th}. Officer of the day.[71] Night with the prisoners. Musings on the unhappy people and the fate before them. Thoughts on the Indian as a human being, a man and brother. His strange history.[72] Inability to fuse with the white man. Difference in physical characteristics between these Indians and the Alaskans. Similarity of some of these men to the Roman type. Alaskans purely Asiatic.

---

70. "Day was spent in forming commission which met 1 PM & adjourned for want of witnesses. Fenn & Brown of Mt. Idaho asked for as complete a list of witnesses as possible in order to identify Indian murders." *Adjutant Journal*, July 17, 1877. Since none of the "prisoners" were even in Idaho at the outbreak of war, Capt. Throckmorton had convened a kangaroo court. Such an obvious injustice to known non-combatants would cause Gen. Howard and future writers (Hampton, Beal, Fee, Wood, Sutherland, and Lavender) to distort, minimize, or delete this absurd event when writing about the conflict.

71. Wood documents his appointment as officer of the day, responsible for "the guard, prisoners, and police of the post or camp." (*Webster's Revised Unabridged*, 1998). This night would be Wood's first extensive personal contact with individual non-treaty Nez Perces, a people he would admire, defend, memorialize, and write about for the rest of his life. For further comment on the importance of this entry, see Smith, *The View From Officers' Row*, 139-146

72. Hamburger transcribes this as "His strange wisdom." Hamburger, *Two Rooms*, 48.

July 18 {–19} [West Bank, Clearwater at Kamiah to Camas Prairie][73]

Breaking camp on return of Cavalry. Surrender of the young wounded "Eagle of the Light."[74] I am improvised a *cudi* and hear the woes and troubles of the innocent captives.[75] I read them a lecture for general effect and say, "So go and sin no more."[76] Night march. No shoe. No nothin' now. Another "bivowk."[sic][77]

July 19 {–20} [Camas Prairie to Cold Spring][78]

Horrible hot stifling march across a dry prairie.[79] No breakfast. No water. Men fainting and falling by the wayside.

---

73. A settler present the morning of July 18 described the river crossing: "The entire day was spent in recrossing. Ten men were taken over at a time in a boat (the one I had built six weeks before.)" Francis M. Redfield, "Reminiscences of Francis M. Redfield, Chief Joseph's War." *Pacific Northwest Quarterly*, 27 (1936): 66-77. Camas Prairie "was a favorite gathering spot for the Nez Perces,...one of the finest camas fields in the area." *Nez Perce Country* (Washington, D.C.: National Park Service, 1983), 196.

74. The warrior Wood interviewed and probably sketched was not Eagle from the Light (Tipyahlanah Ka-ou-pu), a non-treaty Nez Perce chief "who even before the outbreak of the war had become disgusted with conditions in Idaho and had settled down with Flathead friends" in western Montana. Josephy, *Nez Perce Indians*, 573. More likely, Wood interviewed "Temme Ilppilp," or "Red Heart, Jr.," one of Chief Red Heart's four sons. McWhorter, *Hear Me, My Chiefs*, 333; Greene, *Nez Perce Summer*, 372.

75. "Cudi" is a loan word from Latin and/or Arabic for "judge" or "juror." See the *Oxford Latin Dictionary*; *Oxford English Dictionary*. Laura Mosher and Paul Nergelovic, United States Military Academy Library, E-mail to author, April 1, 2004.

76. Here, Wood ironically quotes John 8:11 (*King James Bible*) in which Jesus refuses to condemn an adulteress, then admonishes her — with these words — to change her life. After the "[military] commission could not make a finding in regard to the Indian prisoners," these innocent non-combatants — men, women, and children — were marched sixty miles on foot through heat and dust to Fort Lapwai, transported by steamer to Fort Vancouver, then imprisoned for nine months. Brown, *Flight of the Nez Perce*, 205; Greene, *Nez Perce Summer*, 100, 408-09, n15; McWhorter, *Hear Me, My Chiefs*, 331-332.

77. "Infantry making night march encamped sixteen miles out." Adjutant Journal, July 19, 1877. Apparently, Wood's company elected to march part way to Cold Spring the night of July 18, then bivouac on Camas Prairie rather than bake all the next day in the heat, which can reach over 100 degrees. "No shoe" may reflect the infantry's notoriously inadequate footwear. See Douglas C. McChristian, *The U.S. Army in the West 1870-1880* (Norman: University of Oklahoma Press, 1995). In contrast, "Howard... marched his [mounted?] command 35 miles, to Cold Spring, in one day...." Sutherland, *Howard's Campaign*, 13. Hamburger attributes this night march to Red Heart's band (*Two Rooms*, 48).

78. Intending to intercept the fleeing non-treaty bands in the Bitterroot Valley south of Missoula, Gen. Howard had started his troops for Montana, but before he reached Cold Spring, he learned that the non-treaty warriors had attacked the treaty Indians who had betrayed them, stolen their horses and mules, and burned some property. Greene, *Nez Perce Summer*, 102-103. Wood's infantry company probably camped at a well-known Nez Perce site on Cold Springs Creek about halfway between the Kamiah area and the Lapwai Valley. Diana Mallickan, E-mail to author, March 14, 2004.

79. Refers to Camas Prairie west of Kamiah. Wood's Twenty-first Infantry company probably marched around nineteen miles in full sun to Cold Spring. See Plate 2.19 for Wood's July 20 letter describing this march and camp.

Camp Cold Springs, Idaho Territory,
July 20, 1877

Dear Old Pins,

Otis is in camp and told me yesterday evening that he had heard from a Mrs. Cobb at Ft. Monroe and that you were ill. Some affection of the lungs. I tried to write last night, but it was too dark and I was very tired. (Lights are not allowed in an Indian country, you know). Yesterday, we made a forced march over an open scorching prairie. The heat was killing, stifling, and men were fainting and being sunstruck till we had to dump our packs from the mules to carry the sick. I worked with the sick, wounded, and Indian prisoners; so, as you may easily imagine, I wanted sleep, especially as we had marched all the night before....

I haven't written to you or anybody for a long, long time. I have felt conscience stricken, have wanted to hear of and from you, Pete, and Mac, but my natural laziness, carelessness, and thoughtlessness — combined with studying law & doing confidential work for General Howard in addition to my regular garrison duties — have given me little time for anything but a mild kind of country-village dissipation at Vancouver.... Do get well Pinzy....

I was thinking the other day, during our fight on the Clearwater when the air was filled with invisible humming birds bearing mortal stings, that if I pulled through this, I would try and go home and see you and the old familiar scenes at my home once more. Men were being shot on each side of me, the wounded were writhing and groaning and cursing. The red devils were yow-yowing and war-whooping and their bullets zee-zipping in the grass close to my head, and I felt kind o' homesick you understand. As if I would rather be in the paternal peach orchard listening to the peaceful hum of bees.

I am the most egotistical conceited fool now alive, I think. I sat down to write of you and have scribbled of myself. Tell me first how you are.... It will interest me. I am getting a reputation for being heartless and selfish. If you hear that I am, do not believe that my friendship will ever change. I doubt if I have changed at all. I don't think I am heartless. It hurts me to see others suffer, but I always knew I was selfish....

Come out and see me, stay with me "when this cruel war is over" if I live through it. Vancouver has a delightful summer and fall climate, but a little rainy in the winter. Geary is a happy father, he wrote me of the event in the progress of the human race but I was in the field and have not had time to answer his letter. The foot troop are worked terribly, skirmishing, marching, on picket duty all the time. There I go on myself again!

To return to yourself. Otis tells me also that you and Miss Nannie are engaged to be married, Miss Nannie Smith I mean, of course. According to my code of etiquette, it is very ill bred and impertinent to pry into the private affairs of another; and such affairs concern only the two interested lovers! Until they choose to tell the world, therefore, I do not mean to do more than mention what I have heard. You know (of course you don't know...), I came direct from Alaska into the field without stopping at all, merely changing from ocean to river steamer and have now been since early in March without hearing from anyone, so that all manner of changes may have taken place and be well-known to others but unknown to me. If this report should be so, you know or ought to know that no one can wish both of you life long happiness more sincerely than I do.

I ruined my eyes among the icebergs of Alaska and for months now have suffered a great deal with them. I fear the weakness and inflammation have become chronic. It is on account of this infirmity that I must say goodbye... We move today 18 miles to Lawyer's Canyon to try and intercept Mr. Joe. Mrs. (Gen) Howard wrote to me and told me never to write "Goodbye" at the close of a letter to anyone. So, dear Pins, in spite of Joseph, and sickness, the World, the Flesh, and the Devil, we will say in all cheerfulness and hopefulness, au revoir.

                                      Yours fondly,

                                      Wood

Xcuse paper or dont excuse it just as you please. It is the best I can afford at present. C. E. S. W.

July 20 [Cold Spring to Camas Prairie (Camp Wilkinson)][80]

In camp at Cold Spring. "Throck's" scare.[81] Waiting for the General. The afternoon march and camp on the prairie. Grass to our knees. Rolling hills. Sides speckled with herd and pack train. Men bustling about packs. Reminded of an Oriental camp in some desert, or steppe, and of De Quincey's *Flight of a Tartar Tribe*.[82]

July 21 [Camas Prairie to Lawyer Creek]

March to Camp Alexander in Lawyer's Canyon.[83] Trout, ease, and comfort.

---

80. Sutherland adds: "that night went into camp on the grassy table lands, where there was no wood for fires or for tent poles and the little water...was soon worked into such a mush of mud by the pack mules and cavalry horses that it was impossible to use it...This camp I believe, was named in honor of Captain M. C. Wilkinson, of Portland." *Portland Daily Standard*, August 1, 1877.

81. Capt. Charles B. Throckmorton, 4th Artillery; what scared him is unknown.

82. Allusion to the English Romantic writer Thomas De Quincy (1785-1859) and his famous historical essay, "*Flight of a Tartar Tribe*." Wood may well have read the 1854 reprint of De Quincey's grandiloquent amalgam of history and fiction while a cadet at the United States Military Academy, where he "did an unusual amount of extracurricular reading... [in] works by Shakespeare, Spenser, Milton, and Sir Walter Scott." Edwin Bingham and Tim Barnes, *Wood Works* (Corvallis: Oregon State University Press, 1997), 5. De Quincey narrates the 1771 Torgote Tartars' revolt against Czarist Russia. Relentlessly pursued and killed by Russian troops, 70,000 Tartar families with their livestock fled thousands of miles over eight months — from the Volga region to the western Chinese province of Ili — until they were finally "welcomed [and protected] by the Chinese authorities." While the analogy between the Nez Perces and the Tartar families is incomplete — the Tartars chose to flee — this allusion shows Wood's developing literary repertoire and offers a model for his own later and widely-misunderstood amalgam of fact and fiction about the Nez Perces conflict. Thomas De Quincy, *Flight of a Tartar Tribe*, ed. Milton Haight Turk (New York: Houghton Mifflin, 1897), 2.

83. After praising the trout fishing in Lawyer Creek, Sutherland goes on to explain, "This beautiful camping ground was named after Dr. [C. T.] Alexander, chief of our medical corps, a gentleman of much intelligence and a rare fund of humor which he in vain tries to hide behind an effort to appear misanthropical." *Portland Daily Standard*, August 1, 1877.

Opposite: Plate 2.19 "C.E.S. Wood to Wright P. Edgerton, Camp Cold Springs, Idaho Territory, July 20, 1877."
Recently discovered in family papers, Wood wrote this letter to his old West Point classmate stationed at Fort Monroe near Washington, D.C. At the time, Wood's intended fiancee Nanny Moale Smith was welcoming Edgerton's courtship. Transcribed by Paul Merchant, and edited by George Venn.

Plate 2.20 "Crossing the Clearwater, August, 1877, Nez Perce War." This original pen and ink sketch by Capt. Harry C. Cushing, Fourth Artillery, may depict Howard's infantry around July 30 as they pursue the non-treaty bands over the Lolo Trail.

July 22 [Lawyer Creek][84]

Sunday in the canyon. Arrival of Cushing[85] and command. I am promoted to Aide-de-Camp.[86]

---

84. Lawyer Creek is named for *Hallalhotsoot*, or James Lawyer, friend of the missionaries, head chief of the treaty faction of the tribe. (See Plate 1.16) Misled by white officials, Lawyer arrogated to himself, "the right and obligation to speak for all the bands and to sign away all the lands of Joseph, White Bird, and every other Nez Perce...who lived outside the [Idaho] reservation. Lawyer had neither objected to that act nor explained that he did not possess the right to do what he had done." He died at Kamiah on January 3, 1876, and was buried in the cemetery of the Presbyterian church.... [To] those who were hurt by him or lost their lands as result of his action, he is still considered a man who betrayed the Nez Perces." Josephy, *Nez Perce Country*, 106-112.

85. Capt. Harry C. Cushing, Fourth Artillery, stationed at San Francisco, was "the senior officer...whom Howard was to regard as a capable officer in the future and...2nd Lt. Guy Howard, the general's oldest son who was soon made an aide-de-camp." Brown, *Flight of the Nez Perce*, 211.

86. Capt. Pollock notes, "Two of the members of his [Gen. Howard's] staff are sick, Capt. Wilkinson and Lt. Fletcher, so Lt. Wood is temporarily on the staff. The Lieutenant claims that the pure copper band he wears on the left wrist wards away sickness and bad humors." Pollock, *Grandfather*, 7.

Plate 2.21 "A Scout." Wood's sketch of Arthur Chapman, the controversial scout, trader, settler. Chapman married a Nez Perce woman and learned her language. He led the attack against the non-treaty bands at White Bird, interpreted for Howard, Wood, and Joseph during 1877 and after. (*Daily Graphic*, August 3, 1877.)

July 23 [Lawyer Creek to Cottonwood Creek(Camp Alfred Sully)][87]

Leave all about 6:45 A.M. for Croasdaile Ranch[88] and camp at Chapman's ranch at about 10:45.[89] Nine miles.

---

87. The camp was named after Col. Alfred Sully, Wood's commanding officer, Twenty-first Infantry, at Fort Vancouver.

88. "[Henry] Croasdaile is an ex-officer of the British navy, who owns two large sheep farms here, the houses on each of which were destroyed by the Indians. He is a very pleasant and well educated gentleman, clinging to all of his old English customs even to having a well stocked wine cellar." Sutherland, *Portland Daily Standard*, August 11, 1877. The Nez Perces also may have taken "unusual rifles" and ".35 caliber exploding cartridges" when raiding Croasdaile's ranch, weapons and munitions they used later in the conflict. Brown, *Flight of the Nez Perce*, 412-13.

89. Arthur [I. F. J.] Chapman was a controversial cross-cultural figure. By this date, his house, barn, and outbuildings had been burned by non-treaty warriors, and his horse herd, cattle, chickens, and pigs killed or driven off. In 1861, he settled on the Nez Perces Reservation at Cottonwood Creek. There, he married Mollie (1841-1896), a relative of Chief Eagle of the Light, and Yellow Wolf explains that "he and my uncle, Old Yellow Wolf, had lived in the same house, just as brothers." (McWhorter, *Yellow Wolf*, 55.) Father, husband, stock breeder, trader, Chapman fought against the non-treaty bands, then became Gen. Howard's scout and translator throughout the Army's pursuit. At and after the Nez Perce surrender on October 5, 1877, Chapman translated for Joseph, including Wood's two interviews, then accompanied the surrendered Nez Perces to Fort Leavenworth. In 1879, he translated Joseph's famous speech in Washington D.C., later published in the *North American Review* as "An Indian's View of Indian Affairs," a text declared by Chapman as "nothing more like his [Joseph's] statement than day is like dark" because the text had been extensively revised by A. B. Meacham and others. (Chapman to Howard, February 18, 1880, Howard Papers). See also *Depredation Claim*, Arthur J.[sic] Chapman, Department of Interior, 12/17/86, Bk 2, No. 220; Arthur I. Chapman, *Report of the Secretary of War*. Vol. 1 (Washington, D.C. 1891), 191-94; Robert Clark, *River of the West*, New York: Picador, 1995, 208-9; *Pension Claim of Arthur I. Chapman*, 1902, Biographical Files, OH Research Library; Katherine James E-mails to author, 2001-2.

[Accounts Page A]

Men On Board [caption added]

M. 25 — D. 30 — A. 28
G. 32 — C. 20[90]
            Attached[91]
C.3   Vols. 27 + 15 =42[92]

Rations [caption added]

Bacon or Pork — full
Hard bread — full.[hardtack]
Beans   ``
Coffee   ``
Soap   ``
Salt   ``
Pepper   ``
190 lbs. hard bread due.[93]
2 (½) boxes sardines 2 cans peas
2 oysters 1 clams 1 currant jelly 2 tomatoes[94]

---

90. These initials and numbers may be Wood's tallies of the men and companies that traveled up the Columbia and Snake on the *Almota*. See Wood's June 21 entry.

91. Military term for soldiers temporarily assigned to a company different from their regular command. Apparently, Company C had three individuals from other companies.

92. Wood apparently counted two groups of civilians who volunteered to assist the Army. Because volunteers' numbers varied daily, and because they "were never a stable, dependable part of the military force," it is impossible to identify who Wood tallied here. Brown, *Flight of the Nez Perce*, 149-50.

93. This seems to be Wood's inventory of basic rations.

94. Last six food items — personal rations — were purchased on credit from Capt. Robert Pollock.

Plate 2.22 "Indian Chief." Wood drew this sketch of Buffalo Horn sometime after July 28 when the Idaho Bannock chief arrived in Howard's camp leading nineteen scouts. During the pursuit, Bannocks mutilated Nez Perce dead and threatened Howard's Nez Perce herders. Angry with Howard, Buffalo Horn left to spread the word that — if Indians united — whites could be defeated. In early 1878, he aroused two hundred warriors to attack settlers in southern Idaho and eastern Oregon. He died after a battle with volunteers in the Owyhees. (*Daily Graphic*, August 3, 1877.)

[Accounts Page B]

Clearwater Battlefield Counts [caption added][95]

21 [illegible]   6 Companies
    Killed 6   21st [entire line crossed out]
    134 in the line—6 killed.
    17 men and officers wounded
    11 officers on the line

57
60   674
69   <u>371</u>
21   303   51
21   <u>5</u>
20   255
54
<u>52</u>

---

95. These figures may be Wood's personal tallies after the Battle of the Clearwater, the only combat he experienced during the Nez Perce conflict. See "Chief Joseph, The Nez Perce" *Century Magazine XXVIII*, 1884: 135-42, for his account of the entire conflict. For the actual and comprehensive figures, see Greene, *Nez Perce Summer*, 93.

Plate 2.23 "An Orphan." Sketched by C.E.S. Wood, this may be a stray Nez Perce horse that attracted the footsore infantryman's attention before he was promoted to Howard's aide-de-camp. On this page, Wood records that he bought four horses during the conflict. (*The Daily Graphic*, August 3, 1877, page 1.)

[Accounts Page C]

Dv.[Daily Vouchers?]

Whitford	cash	1.00
Phillipson	"	1.50
"	"	.25
"	cash	0.00
Gen. Howard	"	2.75
Field		3.00

Entered Pollock's mess June 28th 1877 —
Headquarters mess July 22?
———//———
Received from J. W. Jacobs [illegible] 674 pounds hard bread.
    To Norton   19 x 3=27
    [To] Bacon 20 x 3=60
    To Scouts   23 x 3=64
    To Engineers 7 x 3=21
1 horse from A. Chafffin $ 80
2 from J. Miller $250
1 from O. Clarke $125

Sales to Officers
    Bendire 20 lbs hard bread
    Norton 20 lbs

[Accounts Page D]

Bills [caption added]

due Col. [sic] Pollock	$2.25[96]
Hughes	$10.00 paid
Hotel	$13.00
``	$10.00
``	$ 6.00[97]

Credit [bold added]

Myers	$5.00
``	$2.50[98]

Owe Headquarters   18.54 [bold added]

1 great coat
1 blouse [dress shirt]
3 pairs socks
1 pair shoes
2 pairs drawers
1 rubber blanket [groundsheet]
2 woolen blankets
2 flannel shirts
1 pair trousers[99]

[Accounts Page E]

Saddle
Bridle
Spurs
Saddle bags[100]

[End of 1877 diary transcript]

---

96. The grocery list and amount due Capt. Robert Pollock appear at the end of "Rations." This bill may reflect Wood's appetite for delicacies available from his more well-provisioned commanding officer, whose rank he misstates.

97. The hotel expenses may have been for nights in Sitka or Chicago.

98. Loans to an unidentified soldier.

99. When Wood transferred from the ocean-going *California* to the smaller Columbia River steamer *Canby*, his luggage did not accompany him to Lewiston. He then had to buy — on credit — this second set of infantryman's clothing and equipment on June 24 or later (?) at Fort Lapwai.

100. When Wood was promoted to Howard's aide-de-camp on July 22, the infantryman would now be required to ride horseback. That this new equipment is unpriced suggests Gen. Howard may have provided these instruments of Wood's transformation.

III.

THE ADVOCATE: HIS DRAWINGS, POEMS, AND PROSE

General Howard needed help. On Sunday, July 15, 1877, the non-treaty Nez Perces and their huge horse herd had begun their escape to western Montana via Lolo Trail. On Sunday, July 22, in Lewiston, Howard had read in national newspapers that "The [President's] Cabinet yesterday secretly but seriously considered the propriety of displacing Howard and putting [General] Crook in his place. Howard... has made such a sad mess of the campaign...," that it was "quite possible that he will be removed today."[1] Though the General believed he had just defeated the non-treaty Nez Perce on July 11 and 12, he seemed to be losing the fight for favorable opinion in the eastern newspapers — his home front. To make matters worse, he had just given leave to his chief aide-de-camp, Lt. Melville C. Wilkinson, whose health was deteriorating, and who would also recruit Indian scouts among the pacified tribesmen at Warm Springs.[2] Howard could not help himself. He'd lost his right arm in the Civil War and could only write slowly and awkwardly with his left hand.[3] The General needed literate, articulate, intelligent staff officers, he needed someone who could write — legibly, fluently, rapidly, intelligently — he needed someone who could defend him, execute his orders, create his record. Riding from Lewiston to Lawyer Canyon, he realized the solution was obvious: promote his literate judge advocate friend Lt. Wood to headquarters. Already, Wood had been "doing confidential work for Gen. Howard" — presumably the sketches prepared for the eastern press of Howard's "victory" at the Battle of the Clearwater on July 11 and 12.[4] Wood's artistic process — self-described — was portable, adaptable, simple: taking his

---

1. Mark H. Brown, *The Flight of the Nez Perce* (New York: Putnam, 1967), 208.

2. "According to Gen. Howard, Wilkinson's 'gallant services' at Clearwater [on July 11 and 12] resulted in a [recommended] promotion to... brevet major." In 1878, his unprovoked slaughter of non-combatant Palouse Indian men, women, and children near Wallula caused Wilkinson to apply "for an eight-month leave of absence in order to look for a new career" as founder of the Forest Grove Indian School, an institution dedicated to forced assimilation that caused the deaths of many Native American students. See Cary C. Collins, "The Broken Crucible of Assimilation," *Oregon Historical Quarterly*, Winter 2000), 470. Wilkinson was killed in the 1898 uprising of the Pillager Chippewa.

3. Sean Monahan, E-mail to author, June 8, 2001, Bowdoin College, Howard Papers.

4. Wood to Edgerton, July 20, 1877, Aubrey Watzek Library Special Collections, Lewis & Clark College, Portland, Oregon. Transcribed by Paul Merchant.

Plate 3.1 "Mountain Passes in the Bitter Root Mountains." Wood's original caption suggests his respect for the daunting scale and beauty of the Nez Perces' homeland. Completed prior to crossing the Lolo Trail, this is one of five sketches in Wood's second front-page spread. Headlined "Scenes of General Howard's Campaign Against the Nez Perce Indians," the montage was attributed to "an Officer in the Field." (*The Daily Graphic*, August 16, 1877, page 1.)

Plate 3.2 "Canyons of the Salmon River." Wood's original caption names one of two Idaho landscapes published in his second front-page montage. Drawn prior to crossing the Lolo Trail, headlined "Scenes of General Howard's Campaign Against the Nez Perce Indians," the work was attributed as "Sketches by an Officer in the Field." Dedicated to visual art throughout his life, Wood rendered landscapes in various media — pen and ink, water colors, oil paintings. (*The Daily Graphic*, August 16, 1877, page 1.)

pad and pencil, he would find the right place, sit down, and rapidly sketch the subject, then later, he would refine and finish the drawing in pen and black ink.[5]

Lt. Wood's demonstrated literary ability could now help the General in three prose-intensive personae: as new aide-de-camp, he became a secretary who "sat up half the night to write orders and reports by the light of a candle stuck in half of a raw potato."[6]

He composed and copied field orders, messages, telegrams. As new acting adjutant general, Lt. Wood became a chronicler responsible for Gen. Howard's official daily log — a writing task he likely assumed from his predecessor, Lt. Wilkinson. Wood apparently delegated this second role because, on two occasions after the war, he stated that he "turned over the duty of keeping a journal to a sergeant attached to headquarters who wrote an excellent hand."[7]

---

5. Wood to McWhorter, January 3,1942, Lucullus McWhorter Papers, Holland Library, Washington State University, Pullman. [hereafter McWhorter Papers].

6. Autobiographical Notes, WD Box 6(7), Wood Collection, Huntington Library, San Marino, California. [hereafter Wood Collection].

7. In "Pursuit and Capture of Chief Joseph," Wood identified an "official journal which I kept as adjutant in the field" (in *Chief Joseph: The Biography of a Great Indian*, Chester Anders Fee [New York: Wilson-Erickson, 1936],355). In his unpublished autobiography, Wood stated that "I had to keep an accurate set of books that would make history but as when the campaign was over, he [Howard] carried the books off with him...." (Wood Collection, Carton 28-Cylinder A-1). Cited in Part II, Note 78, this *Adjutant Journal* may be the document deposited in the Huntington Library titled *Journal of Expedition against Hostile Nez Perce Indians from Lewiston I.T. to Henry Lake, I.T.* Attributed to Wood, the journal's authorship is dubious at best: the handwriting, except for the title page, is not Wood's and appears to be copied; the first page carries the disclaimer, "Following memorandum taken from jacket diary of Captain M. C. Wilkinson, A.D.E., July 10, 1877." Throughout the text, Wood is referred to infrequently and always in third person. Wood may or may not have dictated this record, but he clearly did not write this text. While Howard attributes such a journal to Wood and quotes from that text throughout his *Nez Perce Joseph* (1881), Wood's original *Adjutant Journal* may have been lost or remains in private hands. An intensive search during this writing did not discover it.

While both of those new roles extended Howard's efficacy, authority, and influence, they implicitly and tacitly generated Wood's third and most significant new persona, "Howard's Advocate" — an imaginative press officer, writer, and artist, who anonymously or identifiably, with or without permission, regardless of audience or occasion, capable of fact and fiction — would speak, write, and draw to defend Gen. Howard, rouse his troops, refute his critics, defend his record, advance his cause. Before July 22, Lt. Wood leaked his first two anonymous press releases to *The Daily Graphic* in New York, where they appeared as front-page montages on August 3 and August 16. Both montages — attributed to "an officer of General Howard's staff" — were accompanied by text favorable to Howard, and the first included a Portland studio portrait. (At this point, Howard needed the positive publicity. Counterattacking, then escaping from Army and civilian forces who attacked them at Big Hole on August 9, the non-treaty bands were miles ahead of Howard's soldiers.) On August 27, the same illustrated paper published Wood's heavily-slanted Camas Meadow article — signed with his initial — and on September 8 his anonymous Camas Meadow drawing.[8] In all this work — his first published writing and art — Wood omits or abstracts all evidence of Army incompetence, human foibles, and humane details.

On August 29, 1877, after months of unsuccessfully pursuing the mounted Nez Perces, Howard rested his foot-weary soldiers, and Lt. Wood composed another text, "General Field Orders No. 6." Writing as Howard's Advocate, Wood offered an explicit and extended defense of Howard and his exhausted troops to which Howard ironically added only two words — "Under God." Signed and dated, this rhetorically-skilled appeal to pathos would later be widely praised, circulated, and published by Army brass and the Department of the Columbia.[9]

Certain they had eluded the soldiers from three different armies sent to capture them, confident they had escaped Gen. Howard's forces, the non-treaty Nez Perces stopped to rest at Bear's Paw on September 29, a day's ride to freedom over the border. There, on the afternoon of September 30, they were attacked and besieged by new forces under Col. Nelson A. Miles and, promised they could return to Idaho in the spring, Chief Joseph — the only surviving and present non-treaty band leader — surrendered to Miles and Gen. Howard — accompanied by Lt. Wood — on October 5, 1877.

Humiliated by press accounts that insulted Gen. Howard or erased Wood and his commanding officer from Chief Joseph's surrender, Howard's Advocate continued his counterattack: first, by persuading the Portland journalist Thomas Sutherland to leak Erskine's "Chief Joseph Surrender Speech" — that begins, "Tell Gen. Howard I know his heart" — to a Bismark, North Dakota, newspaper; then by publishing his own anonymous newspaper articles defending Howard in Chicago and New York; then

---

8. [C. E. S. Wood,] "General Howard's Battle With the Nez Perces Indians, July II; Sketches by an Officer of General Howard's Staff," and "Pictures of the Day," *The Daily Graphic*, August 3, 1877, 1, 233; [C.E.S. Wood,] "Scenes of General Howard's Campaign Against the Nez Perce Indians; from Sketches by an Officer in the Field," and "Pictures of the Day," *The Daily Graphic*, August 16, 1877, 1; [C. E. S. Wood, "General Howard's Campaign Against the Nez Perces Indians; Position of the Camp on August 20 when the Horses Were Stampeded by the Indians," and "Pictures of the Day," *The Daily Graphic*, September 8, 1877, 1; W. [C.E.S.Wood], "A Fight at Break of Day," August 27, 1877, *The Daily Graphic*, 366. See also Wood to McWhorter, January 3, 1942, McWhorter Papers.

9. Charles E. S. Wood, "General Field Orders No. 6," *Supplementary Report* (Non-Treaty Nez Perces Campaign) of Brigadier-General O. O. Howard, Brevet Major-General U.S. Army, Commanding Depart of the Columbia (Portland: Assistant Adjutant General's Office, Department of the Columbia, 1878), 619. At the end of the 1879 reprint of this text in the Wood Collection, Wood wrote, "I am afraid I am responsible for this document — except the "Under God." CESW."

Plate 3.3 "Captives of Joseph's Band Coming Into Miles' Camp." Wood wrote this original caption while in New York, probably at the *Daily Graphic* offices sometime before October 15. After dropping off and writing captions for as many as six sketches, Wood left for Washington, D.C. as Gen. Howard's secret envoy to President Rutherford B. Hayes. Published on November 3, headlined "Closing Scenes of General Howard's Campaign Against the Nez Perces Indians," Wood's last 1877 montage was attributed to "an officer of General Howard's staff."

by distributing more anonymous drawings, stories, and versions of the "Surrender Speech" to the eastern press; then by ghostwriting — as Sutherland — an account of Joseph's surrender for a Portland paper; then by acting as the General's secret envoy to President Hayes; finally, by co-authoring with Howard the heavily slanted post-war Army narrative of the campaign.[10]

Promotion to aide-de-camp ended Erskine's personal introspective diary on July 22, 1877, but Lt. Wood's persona as Howard's Advocate would be created that day, and continue until well after Howard's death in 1909. While Erskine would confound literalists by adopting literary masks, pen names, and anonymity for the rest of his life, he eventually unmasked himself as Howard's Advocate and became explicitly critical of Army conduct, published his disagreements with Gen. Howard, and described his military service this way: "in my youth, I, stupid, fought/Wearing the livery of the State/Whose might is by the richest bought —/A bully which protects the great." Late in his life and off the official record, he referred to Howard as "my ignorant superior officer."[11]

---

10. To track Wood's 1877 leaked versions and revisions of the "Chief Joseph Surrender Speech," begin with *Bismark Tri-Weekly Tribune*, October 26, 1877; *The Inter Ocean* (Chicago), November 9, 1877, 2; *New York Times*, November 16, 1877, 1; *National Tribune* (Washington DC), November 16, 1877; *Harper's Weekly*, November 17, 1877, 906; *Portland Daily Standard*, December 4, 1877. Note: some of these anonymous leaks were probably accomplished with the name and collaboration of Thomas Sutherland. To track Wood's "Surrender Narratives" defending Howard, begin with "The Pursuit and Battle. Semi-Official Report of a Staff Officer." *Chicago Tribune*, October 10, 1877; "The Captive Chief," *San Francisco Chronicle*, November 1, 1877; "To Editor Daily Standard," *Daily Standard* (Portland), November 4, 1877. Note: the last story was ghostwritten as Sutherland. To track Wood's secret mission as Howard's envoy to President Hayes, see C. E. S. Wood to Gen. Howard, November 16, 1877, Howard Papers.

11. "Testament," cited in Edwin Bingham, *Charles Erskine Scott Wood* (Boise, Idaho: Boise State University Press, 1990), 41; Wood Autobiography, Carton 28, Wax Cylinder A-1 Transcript, Wood Collection.

Plate 3.4 "A Smohollo, or Medicine Man." Wood's original caption perhaps identifies a treaty Nez Perce shaman he met prior to crossing the Lolo Trail. Featured in Wood's front-page montage, headlined "Scenes of General Howard's Campaign Against the Nez Perce Indians," the sketch was attributed to "an Officer in the Field." In Wood's 1929 revision of his magnum opus, he briefly described such spiritual leaders: "The wrinkled, grey shaman, by children feared/ And feared by squaws and men, tightens his drum/ And chants reproaches to the angry sun — and prayer." (*The Daily Graphic*, August 16, 1877, page 1.)

As suggested by his July 17 and 18 diary entries, however, Erskine simultaneously became a "Nez Perce Advocate." Admiring Nez Perce courage and skill, identifying with Nez Perce oppression, Erskine rejected military violence and defended the non-treaty bands. His first two montages for *The Daily Graphic* presented — for perhaps the first time in the national press — authentic Nez Perce images of clothing, villages, individuals, horses, boats, and he accurately depicted some of the Nez Perce home landscape. In texts for *The Daily Graphic*, Erskine clearly praised the Nez Perces, "who are, mentally, as well as physically, by all odds the best developed and most advanced of all the aborigines in our Western country." After the surrender on October 5, he interviewed Chief Joseph, made drawings of Joseph and his infant daughter, sketched other surrendering Nez Perces, and published a third montage — all Nez Perce individuals — in New York on November 3.[12] As symbols of their developing friendship, he and Chief Joseph traded saddles.

Though he wrote the first sentence of his "Chief Joseph Surrender Speech" as Howard's Advocate, as Nez Perce Advocate, he synthesized the remaining sixteen sentences from Nez Perce facts (interviews with Joseph), translations of Captain John and Joseph (by Arthur Chapman), and his own observations and fictions (text, syntax, form, context). With this synthesis and persona, he hoped to "redeem their [Nez

---

12. C.E.S. Wood, "Captives of Joseph's Band Coming Into Miles' Camp; Closing Scenes of General Howard's Campaign Against the Nez Perces Indians: Sketches by an Officer of General Howard's Staff." *The Daily Graphic*, November 3, 1877, page 1. At the age of ninety-two and nearly blind, Wood told McWhorter, "The sketches I made... were of the Indian camp which consisted of dug-outs in the hill...and I also made sketches of some horses in the hollow beneath the camp and of some figures of Indians, above the camp near the top of the hill." (Wood to McWhorter, January 3, 1942, McWhorter Papers) A photocopy of one drawing — without place or date — was included in Wood's papers at the Huntington where I identified it in 1999.

Plate 3.5 "Camp of Nez Perce on the Clearwater River." Wood's original caption may identify a treaty band encampment he saw sometime after July 13–perhaps around Kamiah. Wood's attention to this peaceful domestic scene across the river suggests his diary entry on July 17: "thoughts on the Indian as a human being, a man and a brother," and his later poem identifying the Nez Perces as "my brown brothers/Of the wilderness/...[who] instructed my civilization." (*The Daily Graphic*, August 16, 1877, page 1.)

Perce] suffering and the injustice of their situation through the grace and strength of impassioned language."[13] Although neither Joseph nor anyone else present ever confirmed that there was any "Chief Joseph Surrender Speech" on October 5, 1877, Erskine would repeatedly publish, recite, and revise his subversive and poetic oration — disguised as artifact — until that disguised heroic sonnet became the most famous, controversial, and inter-cultural text in nineteenth century western American literature. Masked as Howard's Advocate, drawing and writing without regard to race, Erskine as Nez Perce Advocate had — by the end of 1877 — become the "one officer [who] rejected the fundamental assumption of American civilization's superiority."[14] That transformation is first expressed in this diary.

In publishing his prose after 1877, Erskine probably considered this diary with great ambivalence. Burial of dead friends at White Bird, two "friendly fire" killings, failure to cross the Salmon, a week of absurd marching, jailing Red Heart's innocents, presiding judge of a kangaroo court — these may have been embarrassing weeks that Wood preferred to abstract, background, or forget. In 1884, he did publish "Chief Joseph, The Nez Perce," a full-length pro-Nez Perce narrative of the 1877 conflict which probably drew on his diary (Part II, July 11 and 12) record of the Battle of the Clearwater. In his 1901 collection, *Book of Tales: Being Myths of the North American Indians*, he published two Nez Perce myths collected during those first five weeks of 1877. For the remainder

---

13. Tim Barnes, "Beyond the Bear Paw Mountains: Charles Erskine Scott Wood's Literary Campaign for Freedom," *Sweet Reason* 5 (1986): 16.

14. Sherry L. Smith, *The View from Officer's Row* (Tuscon: University of Arizona Press, 1990), 136.

Plate 3.6 "Chief Joseph." Sketched in pencil by Wood on October 5 and finished with pen and ink before October 15, Wood also delivered this image with caption to the *New York Daily Graphic* while en route to Washington, D.C. as Gen.Howard's secret envoy to President Rutherford B. Hayes. On November 3, six of Wood's original images formed the front page montage: "Closing Scenes of General Howard's Campaign Against the Nez Perces Indians." Later, ghost writing for *Harpers* (November 11, 1877), Wood said: "Joseph has a gentle face, somewhat feminine in its beauty, but intensely strong and full of character. A photograph could not do him justice. A bullet scratch has left a slight scar on his forehead." Answering a post-war request for a picture of Chief Joseph, Howard's secretary replied: "Lieutenant C.E.S. Wood, 21st Infantry at Fort Vancouver, has a very good sketch of him which was published in some of the illustrated papers. If you can get a copy of this, General Howard would very willingly testify to its authenticity."

of his career, however, Wood avoided his first five weeks of marching in circles. Instead, he wrote repeatedly about the last two months of the conflict — especially the surrender he witnessed on October 5 at Bear's Paw. If he told the whole truth implicit in this diary, those first five weeks at war might seem an absurd misadventure of the ridiculous, racist, incompetent, unjust, and ignorant.

In passing, however, many have noted that all of Wood's published prose about 1877 became influential because of his imaginative but false synecdoche. Without knowing or inquiring about Nez Perce warrior culture, Wood — with Gen. Howard's collaboration — substituted Chief Joseph as "the head war chief" for the actual multiple Nez Perce war leaders and their councils. From 1877 on, both Wood and Howard continued to project Euro-American style military genius on the Wallowa band chief who was actually an eloquent civilian leader opposed to war and the only Nez Perce chief willing and able to surrender on October 5. Their trope of Joseph as "Red Napoleon" became widely popular. After sixty-three years, Nez Perce warriors finally corrected this self-vindicating and false image in Lucullus McWhorter's *Yellow Wolf: His Own Story* (1940). Historians, however, still recognize the influence of Wood's imaginative 1877 trope, a fact most recently noted by Jerome Greene: "Although he [Joseph] had not been the leader of all the nontreaty Nez Perces in their historic trek, that perception by the army, the media, and the American public endured, and to a great extent he came to assume that mantle in the years that followed."[15]

---

15. C. E. S. Wood, "Chief Joseph, The Nez Perce." *Century Magazine* XXVIII, 1884: 135-42; C. E. S. Wood, *Book of Tales: Being Myths of the North American Indians* (Portland, Oregon: The Attic Press, 1901, rpt. New York: Vangard Press, 1929); Lucullus McWhorter, *Yellow Wolf: His Own Story* (Caldwell, Idaho: Caxton Printers, 1940); Jerome Greene, *Nez Perce Summer*,1877 (Helena: Montana Historical Society Press, 2000), 357-58.

In contrast to that record in his published prose, Wood did use both events and language from this diary as a source for his published poetry. In composing and revising *The Poet in the Desert*, the hundred-page dramatic poem for which "he wanted to be remembered," he used this diary repeatedly.[16] In the 1915 edition, for instance, he quoted his June 21 diary phrase: "I was a soldier and have gone out to kill and be killed."[17] In that same edition, he recalled his June 27 entry: "I have stood with the soldiers,/Face to face with the great Mother,/And have wrapped the dead in their blankets,/For the long repose."[18] Revising *The Poet in the Desert* in 1918, Wood again used that June 21 phrase but became more explicitly anti-military: "I was a soldier, and, at command/Had gone out to kill and be killed./This was not majestic."[19]

In revising *The Poet in the Desert* in 1918, he also added sixty-three lines alluding to his diary's July 17 entry. Writing as a Nez Perce Advocate in Part XLIX, he praises all Native Americans for their naturalistic wisdom and sense of the sacred, then summarizes the non-treaty Nez Perce bands' 1877 fight and flight:

> I have lived with my brown brothers
> Of the wilderness,
> And found them a mystery.
> The cunning of the swift-darting trout
> A mystery, also;
> The wisdom of voyaging birds;
> The gophers' winter-sleep;
> The knowledge of the bees.
> All a mystery.
> I have lain out with the brown men
> And know they are favored.
> Nature whispered to them her secrets,
> But passed me by.
> They instructed my civilization.
> Stately and full of wisdom
> Was Hin-mah-too-yah-Laht-Kt;
> Thunder rolling in the mountains;
> Joseph, Chief of the Nez-Perces;
> Who, in five battles from the Clearwater
> to Bear Paw Mountain,
> Made bloody protest against Perfidy and Power.
> Ah-laht-ma-kaht, his brother,
> Who led the young men in battle;
> Tsootlem-mox-mox, Yellow Bull;
> Cunning White Bird, a brown Odysseus[20]

---

16. Edwin Bingham and Tim Barnes, eds, *Wood Works* (Corvallis: Oregon State University Press, 1997), 224.

17. Charles Erskine Scott Wood, *The Poet in the Desert* (Portland, Ore: F. W. Baltes, 1915), 103.

18. Wood, *Poet* (1915), 101.

19. Sara Bard Field, ed., *Collected Poems of Charles Erskine Scott Wood* (New York: Vanguard, 1949), 267. (This posthumous collection reprints the 1918 version.)

20. Field, ed., *Collected Poems*, 265-66.

Plate 3.7 "A Nez Perce Brave." Wood's original caption identifies a treaty Nez Perce warrior he met prior to crossing the Lolo Trail. Featured in his August 16 front-page montage, headlined "Scenes of General Howard's Campaign Against the Nez Perce Indians," the sketch was attributed to "an Officer in the Field." Wood admired the Nez Perces' tradition of individual autonomy: "They did not keep order by means of penalties, punishments, or executions. Any member of a tribe...was free to disregard and repudiate the expressed wishes of his chief...If an Indian...should disagree radically with its [sic] chief, he or they were free to go their own way and work out their own salvation." (*The Daily Graphic*, August 16, 1877, page 1.)

In the same stanza, Wood excerpts, lineates, and improvises on Chief Toohoolhoolzote's speech published after the May, 1877, Lapwai Council, a speech for which Gen. Howard arrested and imprisoned him:

> And indomitable Too-hul-hul-soot,
> High Priest, dignified; unafraid; inspired;
> Standing half-naked in the Council Teepee,
> Insisting in low musical gutturals,
> With graceful gesture,
> "The Earth is our Mother.
> "From her we come;
> "To her we return.
> "She belongs to all.
> "She has gathered into her bosom
> "The bones of our ancestors.
> "Their spirits will fight with us
> "When we battle for our home
> "Which is ours from the beginning.
> "Who gave to the White Man
> "Ownership of the Earth,
> "Or what is his authority
> "From the Great Spirit
> "To tear babes from the nursing breast?
> "It is contemptible to have much where others want."

As Nez Perce Advocate, Wood adapted this published version of Tooholhoolzote's speech to highlight the non-treaty chief's protest against the injustice, violence, and poverty created by Wood's civilization. As Howard's Advocate, however, he omitted the key facts stated in Part I: Howard himself ordered the arrest of Toohoolhoolzote and turned the peaceful Lapwai council from a legitimate treaty rights forum into a bellicose, ethnocentric, and racist assault. Wood omitted that his commander failed to grant the validity of non-treaty rights, became intolerant of cultural and religious differences, trusted force to intimidate the parties in a legal dispute. Twenty four years after resigning from the Army, Wood again spared — perhaps out of loyalty — his commanding officer from exposure and potential ridicule.

In revising *The Poet in the Desert* in 1918, Wood also protested all war by making universal his June 27 diary entry:

> I have seen War.
> I have heard it.
> I have smelled it.
> Even now I am waked from dreams
> By the stink of bodies
> Three days dead under the sun.
> Maggots filled their mouths
> And flies crawled over the eyeballs,
> Buzzing up angrily as we threw
> Manhood into the pit of putrefaction.
> Weeds will grow upon the lips of lovers
> And grass flourish out of the hearts of fathers,
> But the father and the lover
> Will return no more.
> Nature will make excellent manure
> Of musicians, artists, artisans, artificers,
> Mechanics, merry-makers, discoverers;
> Poets, makers of soul;
> Sacred receptacles of unspoken dreams.[21]

In the 1929 revision, he added one hundred seventy-eight new lines describing and idealizing Native American cultures in general and implicitly the Nez Perce.[22]

In Wood's unpublished work, the archival record suggests this diary's further significance. In his papers, Wood saved but never published or spoke about his drawing of the Salmon River crossing at White Bird — days that clearly suggested Army incompetence. Sometime after leaving the Army in 1884, Wood may have returned to this diary when composing a long narrative poem about the Wallowa band leaders, and when drafting a Nez Perce War ballad sequence — six poems and one fragment:

---

21. Charles Erskine Scott Wood, *The Poet in the Desert [A New Version]* (sic) (Portland: F. W. Baltes, 1918), 94.

22. Charles Erskine Scott Wood, *The Poet in the Desert* (New York: Vanguard Press, 1929), 134-140. For more on Wood's relationship with Native Americans, see Sherry L. Smith, "Reimagining the Indian." *Pacific Northwest Quarterly*, Volume 87, No. 3, Summer 1996: 149-153.

Ballad of the Cottonwood Ranch

Is it better to die all untarnished
Tho' life has but opened her gates
Or live and grow fat like a friar
With "coward" writ over your face?

We lay along the mountain side;
The Salmon River shot below
The sparks flew upward like men's souls
The rocks danced in the fiery glow.

"Swing low, sweet chariot," sang we all
The laughing youngsters stretched about —
And "Benny Havens," — many a song
of love and war — and many a shout[23]

Wood probably abandoned this ballad sequence — as well as the Wallowa band poem — because the four longest ballads dramatizing Nez Perce individuals came from fantasy, reading, and hearsay. However, the unpublished poems grounded in his diary, such as "Ballad of the Burials," remain more significant. Confronted with mortality that he registered on June 27 as private horror and shock, this unpublished post-war elegy became an honorific memorial for the soldiers — and those who buried them — in Whitebird Canyon:

Ballad of the Burials

This was a man and a soldier–
But now so still it lies
With the buzzards winging o'er it
In its mouth the buzzing flies.

The sun shone hot, the infantry
Did sweat beneath their soldier packs
They sucked their canteens selfishly
They threw their blankets in their tracks.

The sun glared down as he would melt
The barren rocks. He burnt the grass.
The dusty column crawled its way
Toward the White Bird Cañon pass.
(stanza break)

---

23. "Ballads of the Nez Perce War," WD Box 8 (16), Wood Collection.

And all was still where devil din
Of shot and whoop and groan and cry
Had waked the cliffs. But now two days
The dead beneath the sun do lie.

Their faces stare into the sun
The polished flies buzz from their lips.
They lie so still, they shine so white
From boots and shirt and clothing stripped.

The spot is black where splashed their brains
Their bellies slashed with cruel art
And maggots all asquirm do crawl
Where once there lived a soldier's heart.

Hot glared the rocks. The flies swarmed up.
The buzzards marked the hidden spot
Where hopeless all, but fighting grim,
A man at bay had found his lot.

Jerome, the jester, knelt at ease
Behind a rock, still taking sight
But fell asleep till judgment day
When suddenly there fell the night.

And Blacksmith Joe, far up the cliff
Where he had climbed in desp'rate quest
Lay on the rocks, a lump of white
The buzzards hacked his splendid breast.

It was a field of dread and doom
Sown thick with what had once been men
Who spoke to us and were our friends
Now white like mushrooms through this glen.

Here stretched brave Theller on the rocks
Where to the last he stood at bay
And here a-sprawl with ghastly throats
Both Sergeant Jones and Piper lay.

And here the world came to an end
For drunken Fritz. 'Twas his last spree.
And here we swore the oath of blood
To send their souls much company.
(stanza break)

The magpies hop and flutter near.
The little brook goes splashing on.
The sunflowers smile. The blessed air
Is sick with stench of carrion.

And sick the comrades' stomachs are
Who ply the pick and dig the holes
And down, with roar of angry flies
The dead fall in — God rest their souls!

And still, in midnight dreams, I see
The hundred corpses' blackened face.
I smell the smell, and wake for dread.
— It was a very charnel place![24]

In another unpublished poem from that post-war sequence, "Ballad of the Flight Across Salmon River," he continues as a Nez Perce Advocate by expressing his admiration for the bands' skill in crossing rivers — a feat he witnessed and noted in his July 13 diary entry:

Ballad of the Flight across the Salmon River

The river runs foaming and restless
And hurrying down to the sea
Though never a drop returning
It flows eternally.

The saffron east pales into light
The dark squaws bind both bag and bale.
A noise like thunder nearer sweeps
And, tossing head and mane and tail,

Three thousand horses fill the place
A neighing, tossing, trampling throng.
Half naked boys on barebacked steeds
With shrilling screams do urge them on.

The packs are lashed, no pause is made
To drive that wild herd to the brim
Of Salmon River. Then with shouts
Both men and boys forced them to swim.

The leaders plunge and, snorting, swim
And so, with many a cough and toss,
The river is flecked black with heads
Through eddies swift the herd doth cross.

---

24. Ibid.

> The teepees and the parfleche bags
> The bales and litter of the tribe
> Are tied to manes and tails, or dry
> Upon frail rafts of driftwood ride.
>
> The babies on their mothers' backs,
> The children clutch the horses' manes
> And so they flit like passing birds;
> Not any living thing remains.
>
> Down stream and swiftly all are borne
> All straining for the other bank;
> The panting horses scramble out
> And dripping stand with shining flanks.
>
> As rides the last from out the flood
> The first, far on the mountain, seem
> Like flies; then buzzards from the blue
> Drop down toward the silent stream.[25]

Among Wood's many unpublished letters, his 1918 response to an Idaho historian constitutes Wood's only account of the Nez Perce conflict to include events from the first five weeks. Writing to C.J. Brosnan, he defends the Army's river crossing recorded in his June 29-July 1 entries and sketched but never published:

> You say we were halted three days at the Salmon River... We had to cross a mountain torrent in a gorge not as the Indians did, by plunging in with their ponies and little light baggage, but with infantrymen and cavalrymen and a mountain-howitzer and ammunition and rations and pack mules. We got a rope across, by swimming with horses, and then rigged boats of willows, covered with canvas, and I think to cross an army under such conditions, very many of whose men could not even swim, was very creditable even if three days had been taken in the task.[26]

Among Wood's unpublished longer manuscripts, his 1929 revision of *The Poet in the Desert* contains thirteen hand-written, lineated, and revised pages that again narrate the entire tragic story of the Nez Perce conflict. For unknown reasons, Wood removed that poetic treatment from his 1929 text, but saved the manuscript. In this, Wood's last version of the arrest of Toohoolhoolzote, Gen. Howard has just issued his ultimatum: Joseph has thirty days to move to Lapwai:

> Deep was the muttered groan that shook the lodge
> As when at night a troubled cow caught in the marsh
> Rumbles her woe. Too-hul-hul-soot let fall

---

25. Ibid.

26. Wood to C. J. Brosnan, January 7, 1918, Special Collections, University of Idaho Library, Moscow.

His robe and standing, naked, powerful, a
Bronze athlete; on his breast a necklace of
Bear claws with discs of abalone shell.
His voice the sound of a great cataract afar
Or distant thunder, spoke: "Tell him that I
"Am not afraid to die. I am afraid to live.
"I will not live a coward who refused
"My mother and denied the spirits of my fathers.
"I would rather die as a brave man
"Defending that great breast which gave me life
"Which gave my fathers life, and which
"Has taken them back to her rest, where they
"Now wait for me. Is that not better than to live
"Despised by all? Despised by that great breast and
"Those it holds who gave me life — the life I owe
"To them and to that mother? If I leave
"My mother and my ancestors, no one will look
"At me here, now, in the land of death.
"Is it not better for a man to die than live
"And come to that? But if I die as a brave man
"Fighting for all that gave me life, the spirits of
"My ancestors will take me by the hand and welcome me.
"I am for war."

"Ah-ah-ah-ah" ran the approval round the Lodge
And young men with painted faces stirred.
Before the interpreter had closed his lips, the General
As one who stamps out fire, orders Too-hul-hul-soot
To be led off between two guard platoons — handcuffed,
A powerful soldier on each side —
Insulted past all remedy, an Indian disgraced,
The eagle caged, a lion bound.
The long lodge buzzed as when a hive is struck:
"They've broken the sacred council law–
"To come in peace and go in peace, no matter what
"Is said. That is the council law.
"We came unarmed — that is the council law.
"To go in peace — that is the council law.
"Let us depart. It is not good to stay
"When broken is the council law."

The warriors outside crowded against the council wall
Of canvas, straining as eager hounds upon the leash
And muttering assent — "Ah-ah-ah-ah"
But Joseph turned toward his chiefs, dropping
His blanket so it draped down from a girdle of
Dark otter skin — midwinter killed — and raising

His naked arm, naked from shoulder to the waist,
He spoke: "Brothers, we thought the Right would win.
We thought the Truth would shine through all
As the sun shines through a cloud. We hoped
To speak with brothers who if they had lost
The way and wandered in the dark would be
Very glad to walk in the right path when
Came the light. We thought it right that we
Should die in peace upon the land where our
Forefathers lived from long forgotten times
And now are hid in the safe nursing of
The mother breast that gave them life.
But if our brothers do not see the light, must we
Be blind? Too-hul-hul-soot is bound
Because he spoke for war. In council
Everyone may safely speak his thought
And freely go, for that we come to council with
No weapons in our hands. We naked come.
Too-hul-hul-soot is bound for what he said but if
We fight as he has said, we bind the Truth,
The Right. These two unseen are stronger than
Too-hul-hul-soot or you or I or General Howard.
Leave these two free and they will fight for us
And never tire nor run away, but if we go to war
We bind these two and all is lost.
We bind the Truth. We bind the Right. We let loose Hate
Which like a straight black cliff dripping with blood
And not with water will be between us and
Our brothers and they cannot see us, hear us
Nor can we hear them. It is the end.
If we refuse to fight, the black cliff is not there
The sun still shines between us and our brothers
And some day their eyes will open. They will see
The light and give us back our homes.
Not everyone is bad."[27]

In 1940, four years before his death in 1944, Wood again took up Howard's arrest of Toolhoolhoolzote at the Lapwai Council. In revising his 1884 prose article, Wood wrote a marginal note: "General H. remarked to Joseph, 'Too hul hul sut is a mad man and you must make him behave.' As a matter of fact, Too-hul-hul-sut was in the right and General H., carrying out orders from Washington, was absolutely in the wrong."[28]

---

27. [Chief Joseph poem], WD Box 10 (20) ca 1928, Wood Collection, pp. 25-28.

28. [A Memoir of Chief Joseph] . WD Box 43 (24) ca 1940?, Wood Collection. 3 pp. In Sara Bard Field Wood's handwriting: "*Century*, page 136: to be inserted in last paragraph of first column." This is the note at the top of the manuscript page.

This 1877 diary, as a literary source book to paradoxically use and avoid in his published and unpublished work, is perhaps as complex as Wood's later life. After approximately six years as Gen. Howard's aide and advocate, Wood resigned in 1884 to become a Portland lawyer, writer, and civic leader–"probably the most influential cultural figure in turn-of-the century Portland."[29] That same year, as noted earlier, he also published "Chief Joseph, The Nez Perce." Publicly declaring his role as Nez Perce Advocate, his narrative of the 1877 conflict simultaneously elevated Joseph and criticized the federal government for dishonest negotiations with the non-treaty bands. Unlike Gen. Howard, whose July 20, 1880, letter to Chief Joseph shows him rejecting Joseph's plea for help, Wood argued that the non-treaty Nez Perces should be returned from exile in Oklahoma.[30]

In an unpublished 1939 letter, Wood made his disagreements with Howard very clear:

> As to the Nez Perce Campaign, General Howard and I had at least two fixed differences of opinion. I thought he made a mistake in arresting Too-hul-hul-soot, because that was a violation of the sacred freedom of a council... I also differed with General Howard on his failure to protest against the removal of the captive Nez Perces to the Indian Territory... [M]y position was that [Gen.] Miles had promised it [return to the northwest] when he was in command, before Howard's arrival, and that everybody expected it as a matter of course, including Howard.[31]

This difference of opinion can be documented in the unpublished correspondence between Gen. Howard and Chief Joseph. In the following letters, Howard, unlike Wood, refused to help the Nez Perces return to the northwest, even though Joseph's plea for help made the tragic effects of exile very clear.

---

29. Barnes, "Beyond the Bear Paw Mountains," 12.

30. See "Chief Joseph, The Nez Perce." *Century Magazine* XXVIII, 1884: 135-42; Bingham and Barnes, eds., 69-85; Robert Hamburger, *Two Rooms: The Life of Charles Erskine Scott Wood* (Lincoln: University of Nebraska Press, 1998),85.

31. Wood to Edward Lyman, January 7, 1939, Wood Collection.

United States Indian Service
Oakland Agency
Indian Territory
June 30, 1880

General O. O. Howard —
   My friend, you know I have been in Washington. I found many friends there. All the headmen in Washington were glad to meet me. I had a talk with the Commissioner of Indian Affairs. I understood their talk with my heart and kept it.
   I write to you this day. You are my friend, have been, and I think you are today. You are always feeling kind towards the Indians. You know about me, and so do I about you. I am trying to do what's right. I want my people to join me in the way I am going to take. I am now thinking about better things for my people. I never before expressed myself this way or in this manner, so it may be understood by you and others. I know religion is good. It makes all feel kind toward each other. I want you to know now I am going to be a Christian man, so I want you to make known my wishes to all ministers in the West, especially to Dr. Lindsley of Portland, Oregon. I wish you all remember me in your prayers.
   I wish you would help me all you can in my undertakings. What I say now, I say it in truth and it comes from my heart. My people have been suffering a great deal. Since I have been moved to this country, my people are dying off all the time. I hope you will feel for me and sympathize with me and my people.
   I have lost 153 of my people since I was brought to Fort Leavenworth up to the present time, and people are living in a country where the climate is very hot. I want you to know just how I am situated. I remember the councils we had at Lapwai, Idaho. You and I could have agreed if it had not been for other Indians. I regret those days. I now see that you were talking to me right. I am now trying to do better. Hereafter I know I have to do better and I hope all you government officers would do justice to me and treat me as you ought to.
   I know you feel kind towards me wherever you are. I have had same feelings towards you all the time. Let us put away all the wrongs done to each other during the past. You know we are now at peace to each other as friends. I hope we will remain so as friends. We can and all people get along as friends with each other. We all love friendship, so we hope the past offences may be forgotten.
   Then let us be friendly true friends to each other — Whites and Indians. I feel now toward you as my brother and will remain so. Today I take you as my true and best friend. This I say out of my heart. Your body is like mine and your soul is like mine. Your heart is like my heart. You are just the same under our Great Father of all nations. So let us feel to each other as such. I think this is the best thing you and I can do. I hope you take all this into your heart what I have said. You can let me know how you feel.
   So I desire your assistance. Give me your best advice that you know in regard to my situation. I know you will do this for me as my friend. You know more than I do, so you can tell me what is best for me to do. I would do as you tell me to. You told me at the time of surrender that I could go back to my country (Idaho). So I say as you have disappointed me, do something for me now. It will be satisfaction to me to know that you can do something for me, for I know you think of the promises made to me by you, as I have said above. I am trying to take good advices hereafter. I will walk in the way of right. I think I can be happy in doing so. So I am now trying to take hold of civilization. I hope you help me in it. I want your assistance as I have said. You can do this I hope.
   As I say, I and my people are dying in this country and the number I have given. I hope you explain to me if I can be in a better condition than I am in now. You know about these things. You can tell me also what you think since we parted. I have now expressed myself to you. I hope you will say something to me. You will express yourself to me freely as to your own friend.
   This I say to you as to my friend,

                    Yours truly

                    Nez Perce Chief Joseph

writer [and translator]: James Reuben

Headquarters, Department of the Columbia
Fort Vancouver, Washington Territory
July 20, 1880

Chief Joseph, Nez Perce
Oakland Agency
Indian Territory

Dear Friend:

Your kind letter, written by James Ruben, June 30th, has just come to me. I am really glad that you are trying to become a real Christian. I will tell Dr. Lindsly and others of your Christian friends. It will make their hearts glad, and they will pray for you and for your people. I will myself try to do the same.

You still think that I promised to send you back to this Department. I did not promise, but I wrote an order to General Miles to take all the prisoners to my Department in the spring which followed the surrender. I wrote this order because my Division General, at San Francisco, had told me to dispose of all the prisoners somewhere in my Department. I read this order to you, or had the interpreter tell it to you.

But the authorities at Washington said, ... and you know the rest.

Personally, I was not at any time in favor of the Indians, who had been at war returning to Camas Prairie or that neighborhood.

This was not because I was an enemy to you or to your Indians, but because the outrages committed at the outbreak of hostilities were so terrible that I knew that the Whites and your Indians would have new troubles, and nothing could prevent them. In fact, many have been pointed out by name as murderers, and they would have had to stand trial in the courts. If your people had come back in accordance with that order, I should have tried to have put you all at some place far removed from Mount Idaho and Lewiston.

I am your friend, and no longer your enemy. I have much compassion for you. I feel sorry that so many have sickened and died. I know how like children the living ones desire to see the hills and mountains where they were born. But now the soil contains the remains of those who have died, the soil where you are. Can you not make good farms and have good schools there in the Indian Territory? If you can get your people well to work, and make a garden of the land which the Government has assigned you, and if you can say to the children, "Go to school, and grow up contented and happy and industrious," you Joseph, will show yourself a truly great man, and your people can never be blotted out.

James Ruben has returned but I have not yet had a talk with him.

May our Heavenly Father direct you in all your thoughts and bless you, and make you a blessing to all of your people.

Sincerely Yours,

O. O. Howard
Brigadier General, U.S. Army
Commander, Department of the Columbia

Plates 3.8-3.9 "Chief Joseph-General Howard Correspondence, 1880." Still serving Gen. Howard at Fort Vancouver when these letters were exchanged, Lt. Wood never forgot his view that his commander had betrayed the Nez Perces after their surrender. In a 1925 (Portland) *Spectator* article, he wrote, in part, "to corroborate Joseph's subsequent contention that he surrendered on express condition that he would be returned to his own country — Idaho. There is no doubt in my mind that Joseph was led to believe this...." (July 11, p. 7) In a 1929 article in the same magazine, he repeated his advocacy: "I differed with General Howard, who took the ground that no promise had been made Joseph, that the surrender was unconditional, and that he had no right to make terms. I thought this too technical and a moral wrong,... and that we were morally bound." (Sept. 14, p. 23). There is no evidence that Wood publically expressed this disagreement with Howard during his military career. According to Diane Pearson, Chief Joseph's letter is " about 50% Chief Joseph, and about 50% James Reuben." To persuade Howard to support the exiles' return, and to further his Christian agenda, Reuben here contrived Joseph's conversion to Christianity, invented Joseph's false apology for the war, and formalized Joseph's official signature. (Email to author, 8/30/06).

In 1888, three years after the non-treaty survivors returned to the northwest, Wood entertained Joseph at his home in Portland; in 1889, he arranged for the sculptor Olin Warner to cast a bronze medallion of Joseph; in 1892 and 1893, he sent his adolescent son Erskine to live two seasons with Joseph's family on the Colville Reservation. Basking in his history as Howard's Advocate, he received the honorary Oregon militia title of "Colonel." For thirty-four years, he lived in Portland, loved his wife and children, practiced maritime law, defended conservatives and radicals, and continued his quest to be a writer and poet.

In 1911, Erskine fell in love with the young poet Sara Bard Field, eventually brokered a land grant, received a million-dollar commission, resigned his law practice, set up trust accounts for his family, separated from Nanny and, in 1918 at age sixty-six, he and Sara moved to California to make a new life together as writers and poets.

In 1927, Wood published *Heavenly Discourses*, a national best seller with forty or more printings. In 1936, Wood privately confessed that his nationally published, admired, and accepted "Chief Joseph Surrender Speech" was "a literary item" rather than a verbatim transcript — as he had claimed since 1877.[32]

In March, 1941, his June 27, 1877, diary entry — "The alarm shot at midnight. One of our own pickets shot by one of our men" — came back to haunt him. Lucullus McWhorter, an amateur historian researching the 1877 conflict, discovered a diary by Pvt. Mayer in which "Lt. Wood, 21st Infantry, aide-de-camp" was erroneously named as shooting "Private Reed, Troop E, First Cavalry." McWhorter sent a copy of Mayer's accusatory diary entry to Wood, and in *Hear Me, My Chiefs* (1952) published Wood's denial and explanation — in which Wood himself — sixty four years after the fact — confused and conflated Reed's wounding with the July 7 killing of Pvt. Michael Cassidy.[33] Assuming Wood's guilt and adding more guilt because of Wood's verbatim claim regarding the "Chief Joseph Surrender Speech," Mark Brown repeated McWhorter's false allegation that Wood had shot a fellow soldier in *The Flight of the Nez Perce* (1967) and Brown added more hearsay.[34] For reasons best known to them, many subsequent historians — until Jerome Greene — have repeated, let stand, or ignored this false allegation. In his unpublished "Appendix B" to *Nez Perce Summer, 1877*, and recent correspondence, Greene resolved this question:

> I don't think that Lt. Wood shot Reed. There would be something in Wood's ACP File in the National Archives if indeed that happened.... It is possible that an enlisted man named Wood did the shooting. Mayer asserts that it was a picket who did it, and that would have been an enlisted man. Mayer's allusion to Lt. Wood, I think, simply confuses the two [June 30 and July 7] shootings.[35]

---

32. "I took it for my own benefit as a literary item." Wood to McWhorter, January 31, 1936, McWhorter Papers. This statement was also reprinted in various newspapers after Wood's death in 1944. See also my "Chief Joseph's 'Surrender Speech' as a Literary Text." *Oregon English Vol. XX*, 1998: 69-73. For two of Wood's early "verbatim transcript" claims, see *Harper's Weekly*, November 17, 1877, 906; and *Report of the Secretary of War 1877-78*, 1:630. For a more recent and incomplete evaluation of that claim, see Haruo Aoki, "Chief Joseph's Words." *Idaho Yesterdays* 33:3 (Fall, 1989): 16-21.

33. McWhorter, *Hear Me, My Chiefs: Nez Perce Legend and History* (Caldwell, Idaho: Caxtons, 1952), 260-261.

34. Brown, *Flight*, 161.

35. Jerome Greene, "Appendix B: Two Army Shootings at the Salmon River, June 30 and July 7, 1877." Unpublished manuscript; Jerome Greene, email to author, March 8, 2004. See Part II, July 6 diary entry and notes for the second shooting.

> LXIV
>
> **M**an's battle with the Titans is begun,
>   And on the narrow strip beneath the heights
>   Orchards cluster, flecked with sunny lights,
> An oasis from the parched desert won.
> So heavy hang the peaches in the sun
>   That limbs are propped, and children, happy wights,
>   Plunder unchecked with shrill cries of delight
> As in the fragrant shade they laughing run.
> When first I saw where now these shout and play
>   An Indian camp nestled in solitude,
>   I, young moustached, with shoulder-strap and sword,
> And through these hills despairingly at bay
>   The brown men stood, with wives and naked brood.
>   The orchards bloom, but gone the tawny horde.
>
> Going up the Snake River twenty odd years after making the same journey to the Nez Perce War (1877).

Plate 3.10: "Man's Battle With the Titans Is Begun." This page reproduces one of Wood's poems and drawings from *Sonnets*, his collection privately published in 1918. The postscript to the poem reads: "Going up the Snake River twenty odd years after making the same journey to the Nez Perce War (1877)." (See Part II. June 23, 24, 25 for his Snake River diary entries.) To interpret and contextualize his writing and experience, Wood regularly alluded to classical mythology, a stylistic trait most obvious in his *Odysseus*, a one-act play written in 1923. In this sonnet sixty four, he refers to Greek myth in which the original giant Titans (Nez Perces) were overthrown by the new Olympian gods (Anglo-Americans). Wood creates a catalog of ironic contrasting images of change and loss: a young soldier now wiser and older; the quiet old Nez Perces camp with now loud Lewiston; the brown Nez Perces' 1877 despair and fear with the riotous cherubs' innocent laughter and play; the ripe peach orchards with displaced Nez Perce people.

Plate 3.11 "Chief Joseph's Family, Pacific Northwest, ca. 1886." Photographer Unknown (See opposite for details).

Left to right: **Heyume-yoyikt:** Joseph's first wife, mother of daughter Kap-kap-on-mi born in 1865. At Bear's Paw in October, 1877, Heyume-yoyikt escaped to Canada, and Joseph told C. E. S. Wood that his daughter, Kap-kap-on-mi, then eleven years old, was lost during the fighting, but she had, in fact, also escaped to Canada. In 1878, both mother and daughter returned to Lapwai. Kap-kap-on-mi was allowed to stay in Idaho, but Heyume-yoyikt was sent with James Reuben to join the exiles in Oklahoma where she arrived in December, 1878. When the Nez Perces returned in May, 1885, she elected to live at Lapwai rather than to live with Joseph at Colville. **"Little Joseph:** This may be the orphan son of Ollokot, so he is Chief Joseph's nephew. Joseph probably adopted this boy after returning to Colville in 1885, a claim supported by official records confirming that Joseph took two boys into his household sometime during 1886. **Unidentified woman:** Sources disagree about this individual. One historian of Nez Perce exile suggests she may be the anonymous "young woman" Chief Joseph married at Fort Leavenworth in 1878. Alcorns said she was Tom-ma-al-wa-win-mai, Joseph's second wife, whose infant daughter C. E. S. Wood sketched during October, 1877. After her daughter died in Oklahoma in 1879, she divorced Joseph and James Reuben changed her name to "Magdellenia." In the 1885 census, she is listed as a single woman returning to Lapwai. Still other sources suggest this may be Joseph's niece, who was 15 years old in 1885 when the exiles returned to Colville. **Heinmot Tooyalaket:** Young Joseph, chief of the Wallamotkin band(1841-1904). Pictured here sometime between 1886-1890, Young Joseph "had a total of four wives...and nine children — five girls and four boys. All except Kap-kap-on-mi died before the age of two." (Halfmoon) When Joseph arrived in Colville in June, 1885, census records show that his household was comprised of two wives (ages 35 and 32), one single female (age 42), and two daughters — one age 15 and one age 2. Within a few years, the girls had dropped from the list and the 42-year-old woman was also no longer in the family. **Kul-Kul-Smool-Mul**: Joseph's orphaned nephew, and one of the few Nez Perce children born in exile to survive. He was probably adopted by Joseph in Colville sometime after 1885. While living with Chief Joseph's family at Colville in 1892, Erskine Wood wrote that he knew this boy as "Nicky Mowitz." The following summer, Erskine photographed this boy and recorded that Nicky had been renamed "Cool-cool-smool-mool" — an amateur phonetic transcription of the boy's new traditional Nez Perce name. Colville elders confirm that his English name was Willie Andrews Red Star. **Unidentified woman:** The woman seated on Joseph's left may be Wa-Win-Te-Pe-Tal-E-Ka-Sat, one of the widows of Chief Looking Glass. Sometime during exile in Oklahoma, she became Joseph's third wife. After arriving at Colville, Joseph also officially married I-A-To-We-Non-My, the second widow of Looking Glass, his fourth wife (not shown). That last marriage attracted public censure from ignorant Anglo authorities, which Joseph effectively rebuked.

Plate 3.11 Note: Apparently, this mounted photograph was first discovered in donations to the Washington State Historical Society. When it was first published in *Montana, the Magazine of Western History* (1968), Rowena and Gordon Alcorn dated this photo as "taken in the years immediately after the [1877] war." Alcorns used the verso plate, "F. M. Sargent, Photo Artist, Anthony, Kansas" to support their "Kansas/Oklahoma"(1877-1880) provenance, and they interviewed Nez Perce elders at both Lapwai and Nespelem to identify the six members of Chief Joseph's family. Some twenty years later, unaware of the Alcorns' article and the mounted photograph in the Washington State Historical Society, Waible Patton, a Pendleton, Oregon, photographer gave an unmounted print of this exact same photograph to historian Bill Gulick for publication in *Chief Joseph Country* (1981). Patton told Gulick that his predecessor, the Pendleton photographer Walter Bowman (1865-1938), took the photo around 1890 — a statement contradicting the Alcorns' conclusions. So began a continuing dispute about date, time, place, identities, and photographer. Recent national research suggests that this dispute may be resolving. Expert opinions, census demographic data, corroborative documents, archival records, and contemporary witnesses all seem to concur: this photo was taken in the Pacific Northwest around 1886 *after* the Nez Perce exiles returned to Colville. That "Northwest" provenance is supported by compelling internal evidence: fine clothing, unworried expressions, healthy appearance, relative ages, individuals, genders, and marriages. It remains to be established whether Bowman or Sargent took the photo, though Bowman seems the more plausible of the two. (In 1885, Sargent was working in East Las Vegas, New Mexico.) Because the adult women depicted lived over two hundred miles apart — one in Colville, the other at Lapwai — it also remains to be established where the photograph was taken, though Nespelem seems more likely than other sites.

Sources: Rowena and Gordon Alcorn, *Montana, The Magazine of Western History*, Fall, 1968; Otis Halfmoon, *Encyclopedia of North American Indians*; Stanley Clark, *Pacific Northwest Quarterly*, 1945; Erskine Wood, *Days With Chief Joseph*; Maggie Rail, *Chief Joseph Cemetery Records*; J. Diane Pearson, *Journal of Northwest Anthropology*, Spring, 2004; Benjamin P. Moore, *Indian Agent's Report, Chief Joseph's Band...*(1886).

Personal communications: Bill Gulick, Elaine Miller, Jackie Cook and Nez Perce Language Group at Colville: Agnes Davis, Frank Andrews, Frank Halfmoon, Albert Andrews Redstar, James Andrews; Ruth Wapato, Spokane; Nakia Williamson, Cultural Resources, Nez Perce Tribe, Lapwai; Robert Applegate, Archivist, Nez Perce National Historical Park, Lapwai; Larry O'Neal, historian of Nez Perce exile; Paul Merchant, Lewis and Clark College; Normandy S. Helmer, University of Oregon Libraries, and others.

IV.

THE WRITER: A LEGACY OF FAMILY, FRIENDSHIP, AND JUSTICE

Neither false charges nor any of Wood's writing nor the misstatements of historians has ever affected Wood's lifetime record of friendship and respect for the Nez Perce. In fact, Erskine's example — grounded in his diary entries of July 17 and 18 — began a tradition of intercultural and interracial understanding and respect that continues into the present as Wood family legacy.

In October, 1991, at the Congressional Medal of Honor Convention in Vancouver, Wash., the Wood family supported and participated in a Celebrate Freedom Exhibition titled "C. E. S. Wood and Chief Joseph: Brothers in the American West." Featuring historical displays of traditional Nez Perce and Army artifacts — clothing, ornaments, horse gear, weapons, ceremonial objects, daily equipment, and art — the exhibition also included a multi-media program of direct quotations: C. E. S. Wood's writing was read by his grandson, Erskine Wood, and Chief Joseph's 1879 speech was read by Roy White (Kalapoon), a relative of Chief Joseph. In her narrative introducing the exhibit, historian Mary Kline Rose summed up the Erskine-Joseph relationship and its enduring significance: "A mutual respect between soldier and warrior, officer and chief kindled fires of understanding.... [This exhibit] is the story of a flight for freedom and human rights, valor and courage on battlefields in five states, and leadership for justice."[1]

A more extraordinary convergence of Wood and Joseph's descendents began in 1950 when the *Oregon Historical Quarterly* published Erskine Wood, Jr.'s boyhood diary, later published in a hardbound edition as *Days With Chief Joseph*.[2] Documenting his daily life with Chief Joseph's family, the 1893 diary was so popular that the slim hardback was apparently reprinted twice. In 1970, when his diary was reprinted again in paperback, Erskine, Jr. — then 91 — added a four-page epilogue ending with a list of life-long regrets: he hadn't sought out Joseph after 1893; he hadn't corresponded with Joseph; he hadn't asked Joseph about the 1877 conflict; he hadn't told his father that, in reply to C.E.S. Wood's question, "Is there anything I can do for you?", Joseph had said "he

---

1. Mary Kline Rose, *C. E. S. Wood and Chief Joseph: Brothers in the American West* (Vancouver: Celebrate Freedom Exhibition, 1991) 2; Leverett Richards, "Vancouver Exhibits Look at Indian Wars," *Oregonian*, October 3, 1991.

2. Erskine Wood. "Diary of a Fourteen Year Old Boy's Days with Chief Joseph." *Oregon Historical Quarterly LI:2* (June 1950), 71-94. Reprinted as *Days With Chief Joseph*. Portland: Binford and Mort. [1950, 1951, and 1953] 26 pp.

PART IV. THE WRITER: A LEGACY OF FAMILY, FRIENDSHIP, AND JUSTICE

Plate 4.1 "Wood Family and Friends, Fort Canby, ca. 1888-89." *Left to right*: *Seated:* C. E. S. Wood (*petting dog*), Gretchen Beck, Nan Wood (daughter), Captain Merrill, dog, Mabel Beck, Elisa Wood? (daughter). *Middle Row:* Carrie Sladen? (*holding book*), Cousin Fanny Gibbon?, Sallie Lewis, Nanny Smith Wood (bobble hat), Mrs. Beck, unidentified man, unidentified woman (*with crop*). *Back Row:* Max Wood (son), Dr. Walker holding Berwick Wood (son), unidentified Army officer, unidentified younger woman, older woman, younger woman (*with crop*). *Caption by Paul Merchant.*

would like a good stallion to improve the breed of his pony herd."³ A few years after he published those regrets, the 93-year-old attorney met N. Scott Momaday (Kiowa), author of *House Made of Dawn*. During their conversation, Erskine tearfully told the Pulitzer Prize-winning novelist that story of his last regret: failing to transmit to C. E. S. Wood Joseph's request for the gift of a stallion. In 1983, at the age of 104, Erskine died. Momaday kept writing. He did not forget.

In January 1997, twenty-five years after hearing of Erskine's regret, Momaday paraphrased part of Erskine's story in "One Sky Above Us," the final program in Ken Burn's *The West*:

> The second summer he [Erskine] was with Joseph, his father [C. E. S. Wood] wrote to him, through the Indian agent, and he said, 'You won't be going back to live with Joseph any more. The time has come for you to go off to school. You must change your life. Tell Joseph that you won't be coming back, and tell him that I would like to give him a present, a token of my appreciation and esteem. Ask him what he would like.'
>
> And the boy kept the letter until it was time to leave, and Joseph and the boy were riding off to the bluffs of the Columbia, where the boy was going to return to Portland. And on the way, he said, 'I've received a letter from my father, and he wants me to tell you that I won't be coming back. And he wants to make you a gift. What would you like?'
>
> And at this point, in Erskine Wood Jr.'s eyes, there appeared tears. And he said that after a long mile, a silent mile, Joseph said, 'Tell your father to give me a horse.' And the boy was so disappointed that he should ask for so paltry a thing. And he never told his father. And the two men [Joseph and C. E. S. Wood] died. And Erskine Wood, Jr., said, 'I didn't know what the gift of a horse was.'⁴

According to Mary Wood, great granddaughter of C. E. S. Wood and professor of Indian law, "many in her family felt guilty about it [the ungiven gift], especially after the whole country saw the story on TV, and didn't know what they could do."⁵ While the story symbolized the larger failure of amicable intercultural and interracial relationships, Momaday's paraphrase literally documented her grandfather's unwitting boyhood rupture of C.E.S. Wood and Joseph's friendship. The Wood family tradition of respect for and friendship with the Nez Perce had been compromised. This was not acceptable.

According to David Liberty (Cayuse/Umatilla/Walla Walla), a descendent of Old Chief Joseph and a University of Oregon graduate student, he started the solution moving. After learning of Momaday's broadcast, he "walked into her [Mary Wood's]

---

3. Erskine Wood. *Days With Chief Joseph: Diary, Recollections, and Photos*. Portland: Oregon Historical Society, 1970: last two pages (all unnumbered). Also, see the most recent reprint, the "Centennial Edition." Foreword by Mary Rose. Vancouver: Rose Wind Press, 1992/1993.

4. N. Scott Momaday, "The Gift," in *The West*, Vol. 9 "One Sky Above Us," Chapter 5. Ken Burns presents a film produced and directed by Stephen Ives, Jody Abramson, and Michael Kantor. Written by Geoffrey C. Wood and Dayton Duncan. 63 minutes. WETA-TV, Washington, D.C., 1996. PBS Videocassette

5. David Michael Liberty, "It's Never Too Late to Give Away a Horse," *Oregon Historical Quarterly*, 105, No. 1. (2004): 100. All subsequent citations in this paragraph are also from Liberty.

office at the Law School and greeted her by saying, 'Hi Mary. It's never too late to give away a horse.'"[6] Adopting Mary as his cousin, Liberty donated a symbolic quarter to the cause, and agreed to contact his Nez Perce friend and elder, "Horace Axtell, who [he] trusted to make a good recommendation as to who the most appropriate recipient of the horse should be." Mary agreed to contact Wood family members "and start a fund to buy a good stallion." Both agreed that Scott Momaday should be invited.

From the Wood family and friends, contributions began to come in, but their generosity came with some doubt: After more than one hundred years, would the descendents of Chief Joseph accept any gift from them? To find out, a contingent of the Wood family visited Nez Perce leaders in Nespelem and Lapwai and, stating their desire to fulfill Joseph's request, learned that among the many divergent Nez Perces "there was a unifying vision of an opportunity to honor the words spoken a hundred years ago by consummating the gift on a family-to-family level."[7] Encouraged by the Nez Perce response, the grandchildren and great grandchildren of C. E. S. Wood continued to search for the best Appaloosa stallions. They also searched for and found Keith Soy Redthunder, a descendent of Joseph living on the Colville Reservation where Joseph and his Wallowa band were exiled in 1885. Redthunder agreed to accept "the responsibility for this gift."[8]

In spring, 1997, a Wood family delegation traveled to Nespelem to meet Redthunder and to share with him and other Nez Perce elders the information they had gathered on stallions to fulfill Joseph's request. During their stay, Redthunder explained why the horse was important in both present and past Nez Perce culture. After reviewing the videos and papers of twelve stallions, Joseph's relatives and assembled elders finally chose one — Zip's Wild Man. When Redthunder "conditioned his acceptance on a request that the family memorialize the story of the gift, its meaning, symbolism, and purpose, so that all who celebrate in the gift today and in future generations can know its historical and spiritual context," Mary Wood agreed to write that statement.[9] Both families then agreed on the appropriate time and place to fulfill Wood's 1893 promise to Joseph: Wallowa Valley, Oregon — homeland of the illegally dispossessed band.

On July 27, 1997, the sun rose in a high blue sky. Late snow splotched the stone face of the high Wallowas. This was the valley where Joseph and his band had lived for uncountable generations, where C. E. S. Wood, Sarah Winnemucca, and Gen. Howard had passed in 1878 during the Paiute-Bannock uprising.[10] From Nespelem, Lapwai, Pendleton, and Canada, descendents of Chief Joseph — men, women, and children — gathered in a pine-shadowed meadow on the west moraine. Dressed in informal ceremonial clothing, the Nez Perces unpacked their folding chairs and their gifts. A canvas canopy was set up, staked out. Before the Wood family arrived from Joseph, those who practiced their traditional Seven Drums religion "conduct[ed] a ceremony in preparation for receiving the horse." From Utah, the Appaloosa breeder brought the chosen stallion. Helped by twelve friends, fifty-four Wood family members had gathered $25,000 to purchase the horse, trailer, and equipment. In his obituary, the

---

6. Ibid.

7. Mary Christina Wood in "The Gift." Cited in Liberty, 107.

8. Mary Christina Wood, "The Gift," 9. Wood File, Clark County Historical Museum, Vancouver, Wash.

9. Liberty, 107.

10. See "C. E. S. Wood Private Journal, 1878." *Oregon Historical Quarterly*, March 1969, pp 5-38.

Plate 4.2 "Wallowa Moraine." Attorney Erskine Biddle Wood and his daughter, Professor Mary Wood, stand with Zip's Wild Man, the gift horse Joseph requested but never received from Wood's grandfather. In July, 1878, while riding through the area during the Bannock Indian War, C. E. S. Wood noted in his diary: "Camping in the beautiful valley of the Wallowa. Guarded by lofty snow-capped mountains that seem to mourn over the inevitable fate of the Indians who claim this country as their own" (*Oregon Historical Quarterly*, March, 1969: 31).

Wood family noted, "Erskine spearheaded [the] donation...."[11]

Gradually, some forty members of the Wood family — grandchildren, great grand-children, and other relatives — came to the meadow. As one of Wood's granddaughters later recalled, the Nez Perces then formed a half-circle, and "the Wood family joined the half-circle. Scott Momaday spoke about the importance of the horse in Native American culture. A sacred song, created especially for this horse, was sung. And we were invited to offer our words, words from the heart. The Appaloosa was led to the center of the half circle by the Utah breeder [Lynn Walk] and his family. The horse reared. Then, head held high, he leaped into the air with all four feet off the ground. His spirit was big. Tommy Waters took the reins for Redthunder: the horse quieted."[12]

After everyone spoke, the two families formed a receiving line, and as though they were parties at a wedding, the two families faced each other, shook hands, greeted each other, then moved to the next person to exchange their mutual good will. Redthunder, Erskine Biddle Wood (at eighty-six), and his cousin Katherine Livingston posed with the gift stallion held by the Nez Perce wrangler in his black hat, Tommy Waters. Under his domed white Stetson, Scott Momaday stayed cool, visited, and posed for a photograph with Rebecca Wood and David Liberty. Alvin Josephy, the

---

11. Liberty, 104; "In Memoriam, Erskine Biddle Wood," and Mary Christina Wood, "The Gift," 12. Both in Wood File, Clark County Historical Museum, Vancouver, WA.

12. Mardi Wood, "The Ghost Wind Stallion." Wood File, Clark County Historical Museum, Vancouver, WA. Unpublished mss: 2.

Plate 4.3 "The Receiving Line." After the presentation and acceptance of the gift horse, the two families formed a receiving line to meet and greet each other. Here, back to the camera, the Nez Perces — some women in traditional dress — greet some of forty members of the Wood family as they pass.

Plate 4.4 "Fulfillment." *Left to right:* Soy Redthunder, Zip's Wild Man, Tommy Waters, Katherine Livingston (Erskine's cousin), and Erskine Biddle Wood.

Plate 4.5 "Sharon Redthunder with Tom Wood." Braided otter fur, dentalia choker, beaded bracelet, Sharon Redthunder poses with a kneeling Tom Wood, C. E. S. Wood's nephew. Tall, strong, handsome, curly haired, the current Idaho resident resembles his distant uncle whose 1877 Idaho diary is transcribed in Part II.

Plate 4.6 "Two Gifts." During the afternoon, the two families exchanged these gifts: a traditional Pendleton blanket presented to the Woods, and a 1936 portrait of C. E. S. presented to the Redthunders.

PART IV. THE WRITER: A LEGACY OF FAMILY, FRIENDSHIP, AND JUSTICE

Plate 4.7 "The Signing." *Left to right:* Toward the end of the afternoon, Sharon Redthunder, Soy Redthunder, and Mary Wood discuss the event booklet given to all attendees, and prepare to sign the documents transferring Zip's Wild Man to the Redthunders.

aging historian, quietly rejoiced and commended Horace Axtell, the aging Nez Perce elder, for his part in the process. Rudy Shebala and his sons stroked and admired the stallion. David Liberty took pictures, heard laughter, saw a few tears. The Wood family presented the Redthunder family with a framed portrait of C. E. S. Wood; the Redthunder family presented Mary and Erskine and others with Pendleton blankets. As the summer sky darkened, Mary, Sharon Redthunder, and Redthunder sat down in the shade of the long-suffering pines to sign the documents transferring ownership of Zip's Wild Man and to finish the commemorative book. The mountain afternoon turned cooler. The stallion grazed, his mottled black-white rump the color of darkening sky. As everyone was leaving, a lichen-covered stone felt thunder rolling through the mountains and a cold rain laved the ancient witnesses all around. Joseph's 1893 request to Wood had finally been fulfilled. A hundred years of regret had ended.[13]

A year after the "Gift of the Horse" in the Wallowa, the Wood family and the Nez Perces participated in a more dramatic and public ceremony directly related to Wood's diary entries on July 17 and 18 — the days Wood served as judge of the kangaroo court appointed to decide the fate of Red Heart's band. In April, 1998, the first "Red Heart Memorial Ceremony" was held at Fort Vancouver — where Wood lived and served

---

13. This paragraph synthesizes texts cited above and photographs by Suzanne Lewis.

Howard — to commemorate "the hardships endured at Fort Vancouver by Chief Red Heart's band...[including] "the death of [Short Bear] an infant boy." Sponsored by the Nez Perce Tribe, the U.S. Army, the City of Vancouver, and the National Park Service, the first ceremony concluded with a traditional exchange: the Nez Perces presented gifts and blankets to the mayor of Vancouver, to the National Park Service staff, and — by unforeseen coincidence — to Mary Wood's infant son, C. E. S. Wood Fox (Sage). In turn, Mary Wood presented a framed photograph of Chief Jesse Redheart mounted on his prize stallion to the closest male descendant attending — Jesse Redheart. The photo was important: it depicted the equine standard Mary and the Wood family used in choosing the stallion presented to Soy Redthunder in the Wallowa — Zip's Wild Man.[14]

Plate 4.8 "Indian Honor Guard Begins the Ceremony, 2000." Unidentified Portland-Vancouver area VFW Native American veterans present their colors — eagle feather staffs that are the first flags of many tribes. Once representing the counting of coup, eagle feather staffs have become symbols of war veterans.

Since 1998, that ceremony and gift exchange have dramatized a mutual public commitment to healing intercultural wounds. Annually, the Redheart and Wood families gather, attend the ceremony, honor the memory of Short Bear, and exchange traditional gifts such as blankets. One year, Mary Wood presented a potted cedar to plant at the reservation. Another year, Royce Pollard, the Mayor of Vancouver, presented handmade pipes to the Nez Perces. In 2000, "a grove of quaking aspens [was] planted in the area where the grave [of the Nez Perce infant] was thought to be, [and] a birch bench [was] dedicated along with a granite stone that explains the history in English and Nez Perce." More recently, the Woods have also hosted welcome dinners for tribal dignitaries, including dinner at Wood's Landing, the Erskine Wood home on the Columbia River.

According to historian Donna Sinclair's published eyewitness account, the 2000 ceremony began with the traditional presentation of colors, then Nez Perce leaders and orators conducted the four-hour ritual:

---

14. Mary Wood, E-mail to author, April 26, 2006.

Plate 4.9 "W. Otis Halfmoon, Ft. Vancouver, Washington, 1999." Master of Ceremonies for the Red Heart Memorial, Mr. Halfmoon here tells the story of the 1877 conflict. Preferring to call this event a "Healing" rather than a "Reconciliation" ceremony, Mr. Halfmoon is a widely-respected spokesman for and authority on Nez Perce history and traditions. In 1999, he was Idaho Unit Manager of the Nez Perce National Historical Park.

Plate 4.10 "Empty Saddle Ceremony, Ft. Vancouver, 1999." Three descendents of Chief Red Heart lead three riderless horses around the Reconciliation Ceremony circle. Empty saddles on the first two riderless horses represent all the men, women, and children of Chief Red Heart's band imprisoned at Ft. Vancouver. The third riderless horse is bareback and represents Short Bear, the infant son of Little Bear, who died at Ft. Vancouver during imprisonment.

"Uncle" Horace Axtell, a braided Nez Perce elder, began the ceremony with the lilting intonations of a Nez Perce prayer, introductions, and the reading of the names of the jailed Nez Perce.

Wilfred Scott, "Scotty," of the Nez Perce Tribal Executive Council, [then]... explained to the 350 attendees that veterans of any age, gender and ethnicity could join the [Pipe Ceremony] circle and pass the two peace pipes, one of which is said to have belonged to Chief Joseph. The pipes went around a circle passing to Jesse Redheart — a descendent of Chief Red Heart and veteran of the Spanish American War — to the mayor of Vancouver, veterans of World War I, World War II, Vietnam, the Gulf War, and several women.

Nez Perce historian Allen Slickpoo announced...the Empty Saddle Ceremony. Three riderless horses went round the pipe circle led by three mounted riders descended from the Red Heart band. Each empty saddle represented those being honored: Chief Red Heart and the male prisoners, the incarcerated women, and a third, especially symbolic saddle, representing an infant [Short Bear] who died at the guardhouse during the winter of 1877. As the drums droned a steady beat and his voice rose above the occasional din of passing cars, Slickpoo recited a story of inequity, forgiveness, and healing. Another interlocutor between history and memory, Otis Halfmoon, a young Nez Perce historian, related the story of the Nez Perce War to the crowd.

Toward the end of the ceremony, a Giveaway for Friendship and... Honor of Ancestors took place. Mary Wood, descendent of C. E. S. Wood who as a soldier chased the Nez Perce over the Lolo Trail with General Howard, was called to receive a special blanket, an offering of connection between two families. She, in turn, presented a photo [to]...Jesse Redheart [of Soy Redthunder] receiving a long-promised Appaloosa from the Wood family [in 1997]....

Five minutes later a call was made by Wilfred Scott: Was there a six-week old baby boy in the audience to receive a blanket representing the infant who died in Vancouver. As eagles circled unexpectedly above the site of reconciliation, the crowd hushed. Moments passed. Finally, the only person with an infant boy [Cameron] rose, walking slowly toward the group of Indian leaders, tears streaming down her face. The woman was Mary Wood, and in her acceptance of the gift, [she said, "I am truly honored...I promise to always keep alive and teach the importance of what happened here."][15]

In closing, all participants and members of the audience were invited to join a traditional Circle Dance of Friendship. "We hope," said Wilfred Scott, that the Great Spirit is looking down upon us, that our hearts, our prayers rise up to him, that we are in Reconciliation." Side by side, regardless of heritage or status, community members and visitors stepped clockwise to the beat of the drums, shaking the hands of the Nez Perce who circled counterclockwise creating new bonds, new memories and a new direction for ongoing relationships.[16]

---

15. Inserted quote is from Rick Bella, "Nez Perce Ceremony Emphasizes Forgiveness," *The Sunday Oregonian*, 23 April 2000, 3M-C9.

16. Donna Sinclair, "They Did Not Go to War: Chief Red Heart's Band and Native American Incarceration at Fort Vancouver Barracks, 1877-1878," *Columbia* 12:3 (Fall, 1998), 24-33. Note: The above narrative, excerpted from a sidebar on page 32 of Sinclair's fine and lengthy article, has been slightly edited for brevity, accuracy, and clarity.

Plate 4.11 "Planting the Memorial Grove." *Right to left*: Descendents of Chief Red Heart, Don and Katherine Powakee (Nez Perce) from Lapwai, Idaho, planted aspens in memory of Short Bear, the Nez Perce baby who died the winter of 1877 during the imprisonment of Red Heart's band. Credit: Fort Vancouver National Historic Site.

This 1877 diary is more than just the early personal writing of an interesting man with a complex personality. Many historians have found Wood's diary useful because his June 23 entry provides, as Jerome Greene states, "rare contemporary insight into the emotions of soldiers bound for the front during an Indian campaign...."[17] As a literary source book for Wood, the diary proved more paradoxical: it cryptically recorded his awakening — as a Nez Perce Advocate — to racism, oppression, injustice, and militarism, the same forces he had resisted intuitively as West Point cadet. Simultaneously, his diary alludes to major personal transformations — his first face-to-face confrontations with war, death, and mortality and his promotion — as Howard's Advocate — to an ironic position of military and linguistic power. As a survivor of the Nez Perce conflict, he could never forget what he had seen and done. The facts he learned and witnessed generated values and those values generated rights, truths, insights, discoveries. How to transmit those discoveries without betraying both the Nez Perce and Gen. Howard became a lifelong process, as Sherry L. Smith has explained: "Time and again, throughout his life Wood returned to his Indian war experiences as he developed two themes — injustice and perfidy — that played important roles in his prose and poetry."[18]

In the end, Erskine chose friendship and respect for Joseph and the Wallowa band, and rejected himself as Lt. Wood serving Howard's bellicose intolerant ethnocentricity. He learned what Joseph Conrad said earlier in "Heart of Darkness:" "The conquest of the earth, which mostly means the taking it away from those who have a different complexion or slightly flatter noses than ourselves, is not a pretty thing when you look into it too much."[19]

Those choices and decisions and transformations — begun in these scribbled thirty pages — make Wood's legacy essential and contemporary — with the Wallowa band still living in exile, the ownership of the Wallowa valley still an open question, and apology to, meaningful restitution for, and repatriation of Joseph's exiled non-treaty band nowhere in sight.

---

17. Jerome Greene, *Nez Perce Summer*, 1877, 389, n46.

18. Sherry L. Smith, "Reimagining the Indian," *Pacific Northwest Quarterly*, 87.3 (1996): 151.

19. Joseph Conrad, "Heart of Darkness (1902)," in *A Conrad Argosy*, ed. William McFee (New York: Doubleday, 1942), 30.

ACKNOWLEDGMENTS

Since beginning this research in 1996, I've received the generous assistance and ready collaboration of the individuals listed below. Without their answers, aid, and advice, without the support of their institutions, this monograph — part of a longer work-in-progress — would have been impossible. When the full manuscript is published, these brief credits and my thanks will be more specifically elaborated.

Publisher: David Memmott, Wordcraft of Oregon, LLC
Design/Production: Timothy Lucas, Bushwhack Graphics
Cover printed by Herb Everett, Peace Rose Graphics, Eugene, Oregon.
Manuscript Reviewers: Marie Balaban, Timothy Barnes, Charles Coate, Jerome Greene, W. Otis Halfmoon, Timothy Lucas, David and Sue Memmott, Paul Merchant, and Sherry L. Smith.

Editors: Marianne Keddington-Lang at the *Oregon Historical Quarterly* who accepted and, with Joy Margheim, published a short version of this in Spring, 2005; Molly Holz at *Montana The Magazine of Western History,* who granted permission to publish the map from *Nez Perce Summer, 1877*; Jim Hepworth, Confluence Press, who encouraged the author to continue; Tim Barnes and Edwin Bingham, editors of *Wood Works*; Robert Frank, *Northwest Reprints* Editor.

Wood Family: Mary Wood, Sara Wood Smith, and Valerie Alexander.
Joseph Family: Red Thunder, Halfmoon, and Red Star family members.

Nez Perce Tribe: W. Otis Halfmoon, Nakia Williamson, Jackie Cook, Phil Cash Cash, Ruth Wapato, Josiah Pinkham, Agnes Davis, Frank Andrews, Frank Halfmoon, Albert Andrews Redstar, James Andrews.

Federal Librarians, Historians, and Special Collections Archivists:

<u>Library of Congress</u>: Haley Barnett, Margaret Kieckhefer, Bonnie Coles.
<u>National Park Service</u>: Jerome Greene, Denver; Robert Applegate and Diana Mallickan, Nez Perce National Historic Park, Lapwai, Idaho; Theresa Langford and Danielle Gembala, Fort Vancouver National Historic Site, Vancouver, Washington; Otis Halfmoon, Santa Fe, New Mexico.
<u>National Archives and Records Administration</u>: Michael Meier, Washington, DC, and Susan Karren, NARA-Pacific AK Region, Seattle.
<u>Smithsonian Institution</u>: Lonna B. Seibert, Katie McGowan.

Independent Scholars: Donna Sinclair, historian, Portland; Dona Munker, Wood scholar, New York City; Judy Robinson, Bancroft Library researcher, San Francisco; Katherine James, Chapman researcher, La Grande; Larry O'Neal, Nez Perce Exile historian, Baxter Springs, Oklahoma; R.N. DeArmond, Sitka historian; Henry Sayre, art historian, Bend; Ryuichi Yamaguchi, Aichi University, Japan; Karen Savage, City of Vancouver.

ACKNOWLEDGEMENTS

Photographers: Suzanne Lewis, Eugene; Laurence Cotton, Portland; Jan Boles, Caldwell.

Historians: J. Diane Pearson, University of California, Berkeley; Sherry L. Smith, Southern Methodist University; William Lang, Portland State University; Steve Beckham, Lewis and Clark College; Edwin Bingham, University of Oregon; and the late Alvin Josephy. I also benefitted from the histories of David Lavender, Bruce Hampton, Lucullus McWhorter, Bill Gulick, Allen P. Slickpoo, Deward Walker, Francis Haines, and Mark Brown, as well as articles and books by others too numerous to list.

Biographers/Critics: Tim Barnes, Portland Community College; Philip W. Leon, Citadel Military College, Charleston, South Carolina.

Colleagues at Eastern Oregon University: Charles Coate, Tom Madden, Richard Ettinger, Sandra Ellston, Steve Machado.

University and Public Librarians, Curators, Special Collections Archivists:

Pacific Northwest/Alaska

Ken Watson, Katrina Butler, Susan Gaines, Pam DuCharme, Diana Gleason, Debra F. Spidal, Theresa Gillis, Julie Selves, Jan A. Abeita, and Jeffery McDonald all at Pierce Library, Eastern Oregon University; Doug Erickson, Paul Merchant, and Jeremy Skinner at Watzek Library, Lewis and Clark College; Mary L. Finney at Pendleton Public Library; R.L. Schuler at Tacoma Public Library; Normandy Helmer, Will Harmon, and Linda Long at Knight Library, University of Oregon; David M. Liberty at StreamNet Library; Terry Abraham at University of Idaho Library; Jose L. Vargas-Barbery and Robert N. Matuozzi at Holland Library, Washington State University; Gary Lundell and James Stack, University of Washington Libraries; Rose Krause, Northwest Museum of Arts & Culture, Spokane; Dalia Hagan, Lawrence Dodd, Colleen McFarland, Henry Yaple, Dona LaFran, and the late Marilyn Sparks all at Penrose Library, Whitman College; Nancy Lesh, Ralph Courtney, and Arlene Schmuland at University of Alaska/Anchorage Library; Gladi Kulp at Alaska State Library.

West/Southwest

Peter Blodgett, Jill Cogen, Lita Garcia, John Sullivan, Stephen Tabor, Jennifer Martinez, Carrie Haslett, Kristin Cooper, and Dixie Dillon all at The Huntington Library, San Marino, California; Naomi Schultz at the Bancroft Library, University of California Berkeley; Linda Briscoe Myers, University of Texas Austin;

Midwest
Jason Coleman, Cindy Von Elling, Tim J. Watts all at Hale Library,
Kansas State University; Kim Weins, Wellington Public Library, Kansas; Sandy Trotter, Anthony Public Library, Kansas; Sheryl Williams, University of Kansas;

Northeast

Sarah R. Demb, Peabody Museum, Harvard University; Richard Lindemann and Sean Monahan at Bowdoin College Library; Barbara Hail and Mark N. Brown at Brown University Library; William Faucon at Boston Public Library; Jennifer C. Lawyer and Kathryn James at Beinecke Library, Yale University; Karen Campbell and Elizabeth H. Dow at Bailey/Howe Library, University of Vermont; Michala Biondi, New York Public Library; Suzanne Christoff, Laura Mosher, and Paul Nergelovic at United States Military Academy Library; Nan Card, Hayes Presidential Center; Jan Shafer, U.S. Army Military History Institute, Carlile, PA; Kristine Paulus, University of Pennsylvania Museum Archives.

State Historical Society Librarians, Curators, Special Collections Archivists:

Richard H. Engeman, Mikki Tint, Geoff Wexler, MaryAnn Campbell, Lucy Berkley, and Susan Seyl all at Oregon Historical Society; Joy Werlink and Elaine Miller at the Washington State Historical Society; Victoria A. Davis, Jefferson County (WA)Historical Society; Liisa Penner, Clatsop County (OR) Historical Society; Carolyn Bowler, Idaho State Historical Society; Rich Aarstad and Lea Solberg, Montana Historical Society; Jim Ducker, Alaska Historical Society; Karen Meizner, Sitka Historical Society, Tino Avaloz, Minnesota Historical Society; Lesley Martin, Chicago Historical Society; Nicholas Graham, Massachusetts Historical Society; Lisa F. Leibfacher, Ohio Historical Society; Michael A. Church, Kansas State Historical Society.

Research Services:
Nikol Montague at Lexisnexis.com; Tom Izbicki, Archives USA at Johns Hopkins University.

ABOUT THE AUTHOR

In *SOLDIER TO ADVOCATE*, George Venn (1943–) combines his diverse and distinguished talents. When he received the 1994 Stewart Holbrook Award for "outstanding contributions to Oregon's literary life," the presenting official said, "Few people know as much about our region as George Venn." When he received the 1995 Andres Berger Award for poetry, *The Oregonian* described him as "One of the best-known and most respected poets in the state." In 1995, the National Council of Teachers of English recognized his Work with a Multicultural Publishing Award.

In a sense, Venn's thirty-two year commitment to cross-cultural literacy and understanding culminates in *SOLDIER TO ADVOCATE*. That began in 1972 at Eastern Oregon University when Venn invited elders from plateau tribes to address his class on campus — the first such Native American literature course east of the Cascades. For the rest of his thirty-two-year career as Professor of English, he taught, encouraged, and published Native American students, writers, and writing. As Writer-in-Residence, his own publications include poems about Coyote, a memoir on the Upper Skagit, and an address (forthcoming) on the Nez Perce fire myth, "Beaver and the Grande Ronde River." On retiring in 2002, he received the Distinguished Teaching Award from Eastern Oregon University.

In 1970, while teaching and completing his M. F. A. at the University of Montana, Venn first read the outrageous story of the betrayed non-treaty Nez Perces. In 1976, while teaching at the Chief Joseph Summer Seminar in Wallowa County, Venn heard Alvin Josephy tell that tragic story again. Years later, while serving as General Editor of the nationally-praised *OREGON LITERATURE SERIES*, he became acquainted with the life and writing of Charles Erskine Scott Wood. Drawn by Wood's complex relationship with Joseph, Venn has written and lectured about Wood's writing since 1995.

Distinguished alumnus of Albertson College of Idaho, Venn is the author of four other books, most recently *WEST OF PARADISE*, finalist for an Oregon Book Award. In 2005, his collection, *MARKING THE MAGIC CIRCLE* was selected by the Oregon Cultural Heritage Commission as one of the 100 best Oregon books in the past two hundred years. "Forgive Us...," a poem published in *OFF THE MAIN ROAD*, was awarded a Pushcart Prize, and other poems have been anthologized in seventeen different state, regional, and national collections. His prose has been published in more than thirty different periodicals and anthologized in sixteen collections. He now lives and writes in the Grande Ronde Valley.